THE PLAN OF YOUR LIFE

managing what matters most

DR. CHRIS STEPHENS

DCS Publishing
10740 Faith Promise Lane
Knoxville, TN 37931

First Edition, 2011

ISBN 978-0-9817812-3-5

Cover design by Kate Moore, katemoorecreative.com
Book layout by Heather Burson, heatherbursondesign.com
Author photo © Shanell Bledsoe, bledsoephotography.com

Printed in the United States of America

Foreword

I'll never forget the long summer day between my sophomore and junior year of college. It started like any normal day. In fact, I remember Brandi and I had been dating a little over a year and we were actually babysitting her cousins who were in town.

The news reports had been floating around for days that O. J. Simpson was a possible suspect in the killing of his ex-wife. Then the event happened that caught the nation's attention. O. J. driving in that infamous white Bronco down the interstate as dozens of LA policemen were in pursuit.

We sat there in shock as we watched for hours this entire event unfolding on national television. I remember just shaking my head and thinking, "No way." How could this guy be so stupid? He's got money, fame, and just about anything else a person could want. How could he spiral like this?

Like most people, I'll never forget where I was and what I was doing when I heard the news of such events as the one I just mentioned, as well as Princess Diana's fatal car wreck, John F. Kennedy, Jr.'s plane crash, or Michael Jackson's overdose.

Each one of these events had me glued to the television as I watched the reports unfold. There are probably a variety of psychological reasons these events captured my attention, but one major theme is that in some way I thought they had the good life. I thought they had such a "good life" that this surely couldn't be happening to them.

I experienced the exact same thing while recently watching Tiger Woods' very put together life unwrap in front of all of us. We're fascinated because often we think that if we had all the good stuff the celebrity had then we would be smarter; we would be able to enjoy the good life.

No you wouldn't. Don't fool yourself. You see, the problem is that what you've been convinced is the "good life," really isn't the good life at all. The problem is all the money, talent, attractiveness, and popularity in the world will not protect you from the stupidity of sin. All of those things will not fulfill the desire you have burning in your life for more.

Dallas Willard says there is a fundamental question every human being is asking: "Who has 'the good life'?"

This is an important question because at the end of the day you will pursue what you have determined to be the "good life."

As I started to read the manuscript that led to the book you now hold in your hands, I began to realize just what an amazing resource Pastor Chris is sharing with us. This is not only a book that will help you discover the "good life," but it will actually tell you how to achieve it, if you really want it.

Much of the genius of this book undoubtedly lies in the reality that Pastor Chris has lived these principles out. I've had the unbelievable privilege of having Pastor Chris not only be a mentor to me, but a good friend and my life is better for it. I can tell you first hand that if you'll listen to the God-given wisdom he shares in this book, your life will never be the same.

I am deeply grateful for the transformation that has happened in my life as a result of the information in this book and I hope most earnestly it will be so for you as well.

This is your life.

This is your plan.

Don't just read this book. Live it out. Allow the God of grace to lead you and guide you through each chapter. Do the exercises, and fill out the forms. Don't rush, but soak it in. You won't regret it, for the "good life" is just around the corner.

Pete Wilson,
Lead Pastor of Cross Point Church, Speaker and Author of Plan B

Through the creative use of an entertaining story, Chris Stephens has conveyed life lessons in an understandable and implementable format. Discovering our life purpose is only part of the process. We must have a plan and pursue our life purpose with a focused passion. Dr. Stephens is no mere teacher of truth. I have been watching his life for more than thirty years. I know him to be a practitioner and learner. He has learned and applied the principles he shares in this book in his own laboratory of life. Understand your purpose, make a plan, work your plan and watch what God will do in the exciting journey of your life.

—Dr. John O. Yarbrough
Former Executive Vice President of the International Mission Board

Each of us needs motivation, challenge, and a plan for "life growth." In The Plan of Your Life, Chris Stephens has given us a practical, comprehensive, biblical, and executable approach for personal growth. With creativity and sensitivity he has delivered this valuable plan for you to own, read, digest, and follow. You will be on the road to a better biblical future with this guide by your side!

—Dr. Claude Thomas
Executive Director of C3 Global

Chris is one of the finest leaders I have had the privilege to mentor. I have watched him grow a great church in Louisiana and now in Tennessee. Chris has been used to raise up a new generation of leaders. It has been great to watch him grow.

—Dr. John Maxwell
Founder of EQUIP and INJOY Stewardship Services

Acknowledgements

I'm not sure how acknowledgement pages began, but they are almost as difficult to write as the book itself. Who do you thank? Who did you miss? With that said, here goes. I'm grateful for Jesus and His death for us, and for the life and potential He placed in us. I am so grateful for mentors throughout my spiritual journey like John Yarbrough, my first pastor, and many others who followed him. For my wife, Michele; she is my greatest cheerleader. I'm thrilled by the support my family continues to give me. For the staff at Faith Promise, the church I pastor. For Gloria, my tireless assistant of 15 years, who has proofed this manuscript too many times to count. For Josh Whitehead, who pushes me more than any person alive. For Chuck Carringer, who is a constant encourager and friend. I also want to thank my son, Micah. My close bond with him gave me the creativity to write this book. I am surrounded by people who love me and pray for God's best in my personal growth. I am the most blessed man alive. How cool to be God's favorite!

Contents

INTRODUCTION

"For I know the plans I have for you," declares the Lord,
"plans to prosper you and not to harm you, plans to give
you hope and a future."
— *Jeremiah 29:11 (NIV)*

There's nothing more futile in life than sitting around waiting for God to do something.

It's certainly not that He can't. The problem is on the receiving end—we just don't employ the solutions He has given.

God gives us, "all things richly to enjoy" (1 Timothy 6:17, paraphrased). He has also given us, "power to make wealth" (Deuteronomy 8:18). He has given us a plan for abundant life in His Word—principles of sowing and reaping, giving and receiving, working and enjoying the fruit of it. Following the plan isn't a matter of sitting on our hands and letting the blessings fall. It requires action, since faith without works is dead.

> Following the plan isn't a matter of sitting on our hands and letting the blessings fall.

Unsatisfied people don't realize that what they need is a plan. And the plan is there, in the context of the Bible. But for a depressed, despondent or discouraged individual, it can take years to sift it out. That's why I've written this book—to help you get going. I've pulled out some of the most basic principles of success and applied them within a framework of fiction so it won't feel like work!

I think you'll be able to identify with my story about Mike. He's really every man. And every woman. He's the guy or gal who spins his or her wheels trying to find success the world's way. But then God offers him or her an opportunity. It's a chance for him or her to gain some traction; a chance to choose whether he or she will get a life or just sit back down and dream.

Following a plan sounds confining, but it's really the key to freedom. By actively applying the principles of ordering your life, you'll soon find the satisfaction that I have discovered in my own life. I apply these principles daily, and they have enriched my life in every area. I want to share that with you!

So grab a latte, find a comfortable chair, and join Mike on his journey of discovery. It's *The Plan of Your Life*!

Pastor Chris

Aiming at Nothing Equals
a Bull's Eye Every Time

Dad was making his way toward me, coursing through a sea of black mortarboards and tassels. His eagerness was so visible, but he restrained himself, gently guiding Mom with a hand on her shoulder as he let her lead the way. And he had that look—the building smile he couldn't suppress. His cheeks rose, pressing his eyes into a twinkle. It was the look he had the day I was baptized, when I was twelve.

Dad was proud, I could tell. I tucked the black leather portfolio under my left arm so he could shake my hand, and I startled myself by the move. For a moment I felt just like him; he always used to tuck his black leather Bible under his arm so he could greet folks after church. I'd never been conscious of that before, but here I was, suddenly feeling like a picture of the man I admired more than any other. Perhaps, at last, I had become my dad.

I moved toward the little herd of people who were coming to congratulate me—Mom and Dad, my younger brother Zeke, my sister Candice, and her husband Frankie carrying Dad's namesake, Caleb. My aunt and uncle followed behind them. I hugged my mom, who was wiping her beaming eyes with a tissue, and I held out my hand to Dad in the traditional manly fashion, but he grabbed me instead and gave me the biggest bear hug I can remember.

Clutched in his strong arms, I heard Dad's voice so close to my ear, *"I'm proud of you, Son. I know you've worked hard for this."* Then he pulled back to look at me, patted my shoulders firmly, and dammed up a river of emotion. *"God is going to do great things with your life, Son!"* Those words set my teeth on edge. It was too much expectation. What if nothing ever became of my life? What if I couldn't get a job—a full-time job? What if I would never do anything more than what I was doing, which was nothing, in my opinion. Part-time teller at a dying, independent bank. I was afraid of failure, and all I could see in my future was another two years of grad school, going for my Ph.D. Perhaps, during that time, I'd actually get a vision for where I was going. And perhaps I'd even gain confidence in myself.

> "God is going to do great things with your life, Son!"

The moments after Dad's words were a blur of smiles and hugs and lively chatter. Everyone was so happy; Dad, in particular, was so proud.

When the congratulations subsided and clusters of people went their separate ways from campus, Mom, Dad and the others drove to Melvin and Joyce's house on the edge of town, where I planned to join them after a goodbye dinner with some of my college buddies. Dad had joked about the degree costing six years of my life and took the diploma for safekeeping. We planned to have some of Aunt Joyce's famous homemade ice cream later on, so I was warned not to order dessert.

It was in the middle of dinner when I felt my cell phone vibrating silently in my pocket. I looked at the number—why would Uncle Melvin be calling me? It was ill-timed, but I thought I should take the call.

"Mike, it's Uncle Melvin." His voice was stressed and tight. The restaurant banter rose, and at first, I couldn't make out what he

was saying. Something about Dad. I got up and moved away from the laughter.

"Melvin, you're breaking up—what did you say?"

"Your dad is on the way to the hospital—by ambulance. He just collapsed, just fell over here at the house...I don't know what happened...he wasn't breathing."

I knew then what people mean when they say their blood ran cold. I felt a shiver run through me that seemed to come straight out of another world. I couldn't believe a man so strong could just collapse. *"Is he okay? I mean, is he going to be all right? Wait—wa... is ...Where's Mom?"* I fumbled for my keys and my wallet. My friend Brett, sensing a crisis, quickly laid down a wad of bills to cover our meals and followed me out the door.

"I don't know if it's a heart attack or what," Melvin said, his voice shaking. *"Your mom went with him in the ambulance—she's pretty much a wreck and asked me to call you. God...Lord Jesus...we need to pray, Mike..."*

It took one second to descend from the heights of celebration to the depths of despair. I believe my heart missed a few beats and my stomach became a knot, gnarling and pulling, drawing stubborn tears. All I could do was race to my car. I was somehow able to relay the basics to Brett, who went back and told the others what was happening.

Once in the car alone, I began to fall apart. *"Please God, I need my dad!"* I was almost begging. No, I *was* begging. I cried out to God for all I was worth. I had never prayed so hard in all my life. Suddenly, I became aware of all my spiritual shortcomings, my inconsistencies, my basic unworthiness. Why should God listen to me? I had hardly spoken to God at all for nearly four years. My breakup with Allison Jaynes two years before had sealed the deal. I had grown bitter and dead inside and just plunged headlong into my master's program. For the moment, all the bitterness—even the stupid girlfriend drama—seemed so meaningless. Now I needed God, but I didn't feel I had an in. My dad's life was possibly hanging by a thread. Perhaps he was even gone already. Would God hear me? The sudden anxiety drove me to instinctively grab my cell phone to call the one person I would look to for help—but I couldn't call Dad about this one. For the first time ever, Dad was unavailable.

When I got to the hospital, I was led to a family waiting area burgeoning with people. How could anyone have gotten there before me? I had virtually flown through traffic. But there they were—tons of people. It was obvious my dad had a lot of friends. As I made my way into the room, nobody said a word. The people just parted like the Red Sea, until I saw Mom standing on the other side. Her brow was arched like a little girl, lost. My brother's face was buried in her neck, and Candice just stood there, wide-eyed, with her hands to her mouth, suppressing all sound in her moment of utter disbelief. The fears I'd sought to escape on the 30-minute drive were overtaking me, devouring me. I did not need to ask. The answer was on every face in the room. As my eyes locked with Mom's, I could read her lips, *"He's gone."* With that, she and Zeke both fell into my arms sobbing. What could I do? Dad can't be gone! No, God! This is not fair! Hot tears burned my face as they rolled down my cheeks and soaked the shoulder of my mother's pink shirt. Candice released a plaintive wail and crumbled into Frankie's arms, and with that, the rest of the crowd seemed to receive their permission to weep. The world seemed to end. Mom and I clung to each other for dear life, life lost. I was stuck in a nightmare, wasn't I? Reality seemed to be running ahead of me and I wanted to call it back. I just couldn't grasp what was happening. Life was out of my control.

It felt so strange to be so intimate with my family again. I couldn't find my place, emotionally. At home, as the middle child and the eldest son, Dad had always counted on me to handle things when he was away. But he was never gone for more than a week or two for a conference or a short-term volunteer mission to places such as the Amazon regions of Brazil. Now the family was facing the ultimate crisis—Dad was gone forever, and I could do nothing but hold my mother. Not as her consoler, as some may have perceived, but as a wounded son. I needed her so badly, but knew she needed me more, I had to hold myself together, put my horrific grief aside and comfort my mom. That's what Dad would have expected of me.

The next few days were a blur—caskets, flowers, church ladies with crock pots. I made most of the funeral arrangements with Candice. Zeke, at 21, had never even purchased an iPod without Dad's help. Making funeral arrangements was completely out of his league. My heart went out to him as he attempted to share the load and sound knowledgeable to the funeral director. As for Mom, she wasn't doing very well; it was all she could do to receive tubs of fried chicken at the door and graciously feign interest in conversation.

At the funeral the pastor said the service was a celebration of a life well lived. Celebration? It sounded so inappropriate to me. I sure didn't feel like celebrating—or eating, for that matter. Dad was right—he used to joke that when someone passes away you should expect to go to the gravesite and come back and eat fried chicken and potato salad until you feel better. Comfort food, they call it. Is there really any comfort in a plastic plate of greasy carbs and a broken fork when you've lost your dad, your best friend?

Pastor said that Dad was a devout Christ-follower and was now in heaven. I had always thought I believed in heaven. But now it seemed as mythical as Santa's North Pole headquarters. The horrors of death seemed to mock any ideas I had of heaven. Dad did not look very angelic in his bronze box, surrounded by sprays of yellow gladiolus and carnations dyed turquoise. Those arrangements with the palm fronds and shiny paper ribbons only seem to be used to grace the settings of the dead and I wondered why people kept using them. The church reeked of the cut flowers and pollens, and Dad in his make-up looked like a figure in a wax museum—only a semblance of the man I knew. That visage, the smells, and the doleful music bore no connection to heaven for me whatsoever. It made me sick.

But then friends, relatives and colleagues began sharing their memories of the man they admired more than any other. Uncle Melvin got up and told a story I'd long forgotten. It was something that happened when I was about seven years old. Dad had given us kids five-gallon buckets with the fatherly command to clean up the yard—four flat acres in southwest Louisiana. That yard always looked as big as the state to me. Soon after we started it began to rain. Candice and Zeke bailed out and sneaked into the house. They slipped through the back door and crept up the steps in an attempt to avoid detection by Dad's radar ears. Of course, he heard them anyway and was amused that they thought they had to sneak in to get out of working in the rain. He figured all three of us had come in, so he just sat reading the paper, enjoying the sounds of a gentle shower and the distant rumble of thunder. But about 30 minutes later, my absence manifested, and the whole family started to look for me. Mom realized I was still outside just as lightning exploded across the blackened Louisiana sky. There was a tremendous clap of thunder, heralding a gush of rain pouring as it only can in the bayou. Dad looked out the front bay window and saw his indomitable little son picking up paper and debris that was blowing all over the yard in the storm. He rushed out into the deluge and scooped me up, his eyes as flooded as the gutter above the door. I had committed to work until my task was completed. I don't even remember that day. But Uncle Melvin said that Dad was deeply proud of his "little man."

I sat in the pew, crushed by the memory that I had made him proud—and the painful reminder that my intense need to please him was rooted so far back in my life. All I ever wanted to do was make him proud of me. And the possibility of letting him down was terrifying.

Dad seemed to know how to succeed at whatever his hand found to do. He had a successful freight company. He owned an impressive fleet of trucks, employed drivers in three states; and more than 300 people depended on him for work. He had four offices, including a sizeable local office staff, and each one of those locals was present—and weeping openly—at his funeral.

An appointments clerk told how Dad had knelt and prayed with her at her desk one day when he heard that her daughter had run away from home. Some dockworker named Carl remembered how Dad sent one of the company mechanics to his house to fix the alternator on his wife's car when Carl was laid up with appendicitis. Then one of the night janitors even remarked about how Dad so kindly left each of them a huge fruit and cheese basket next to the vacuum cleaners at Christmastime—in addition to their bonuses. And a grateful truck driver recalled how he had spilled oil all over his shirt doing a repair, right before an urgent call came in that his wife was about to give birth to their son. Dad, being the same size, cheerfully took off his own shirt so the man wouldn't have to waste a single moment going home first. That was Dad. He would literally give you the shirt off his back. No wonder everybody loved him.

The stories told that day at the funeral made me laugh, they made me cry; they made me proud to be his son. I had no idea how many lives had been touched by the kindness of my dad. People I'd never heard of seemed to have a special, intimate story to tell. And after the service, the reception line seemed as long as the Mississippi River. We had to sit Mom down in a chair.

A few days after the funeral, Josh Witherington, the president of Dad's company, called me and said we needed to meet as soon as I was able. I thought it was just an obligatory gesture of kindness. He was a good friend of Dad's, and I figured he was doing the brotherly thing, checking up on the family, seeing how things were faring for Mom. We met for lunch at a nice downtown restaurant where he had a rather private booth reserved. Dad's attorney, Allen Brock, was already seated there, waiting for us. I began to get the idea that this was no fluffy, token lunch meeting, and I was a little nervous about it. I wondered whether Dad's company was in some kind of trouble. We ordered our meals, and Josh actually asked God to bless the meal and the meeting as well. I was a little relieved, but also surprised. I thought only Dad did things like that.

"Mike, you're a smart man, and I see no reason to tiptoe around this," Josh said. *"Your dad...he had some wishes regarding the company. That's why Allen is here. It's kind of a legal thing...well, that's an understatement...it IS a legal thing. But it's what your dad wanted, so it's also personal."*

I was confused.

"Josh, you're wearing those toe-shoes...ballet is not your forte. Cut some rug," Allen jested.

"Okay, I said I'd get to it, so here it is. Mike, your dad wanted you to take over Montgomery Freight as CEO. He left me specific instructions in case anything ever happened to him."

I was stunned. I could barely speak. *"What? You must be kidding!"*

"It's part of the will," said Allen. *"Caleb wanted you to carry on for him."*

"But I don't know anything about trucking."

"Mike, you're probably more qualified than your dad ever was! You've got an M.B.A.—he had an associate's degree. You were at the top of your class—you won the Pennington Award. I think you know something about business."

"Yeah, but actually doing it is...uh...it's..."

I think Josh actually rolled his eyes at my hesitancy. At least he shook his head in disbelief. *"Most kids your age—pardon me, most young men your age would jump at a chance like this. We're talking CEO of a multi-million dollar operation here, with offices in three* states. *You just graduated. You don't have a job, or a job prospect. Here's the chance of a lifetime being dropped in your lap. And besides that, it's your father's will."*

"*I know, I know…it's just…not what I saw myself doing with my life."*

"*What's really the issue, Mike?"* Allen asked. "*You have all the makings of a promising businessman—education, drive…what's holding you back?"*

I couldn't answer. I just froze. I'd worked all my life to impress my dad, and now I had the chance to step right into his shoes. But I couldn't fill them. I was not the man he thought I was.

Josh was frustrated. "*I don't know what to tell you—your dad thought you were ready. He was explicit in his instructions. What am I supposed to do with this?"*

Allen cut in. "*You don't have to decide anything today, Mike. The company is holding its own for the moment. Why don't you just take a few days and think about it. Meanwhile—"*

He pulled a large manila envelope out of his laptop case.

"*You can go over this."* He handed me the envelope.

"*What is it?"* I asked.

"*It's a letter from your dad."*

"*To me?"*

"*To you. He wrote it several months ago."*

I felt prickles go down my spine and the sides of my calves. A letter—from my dad! "*Are you serious? This is like something out of The Twilight Zone!"*

"Funny you should mention movies. There's also a DVD," Allen explained. *"Your dad put this together for you after that heart episode in Rochester last year. It scared him—not the dying part; he was clear about that. He was just afraid that he hadn't done everything he could as a father to prepare you. He had a lot to say, and thought it would be best just to put it down on video. He was never much of a writer. Oh, and he wanted you to watch it in his office, sitting in his chair. Kinda quirky maybe, but that was Caleb...he did things a little differently."*

Yes, that was Dad. Different. He didn't conform to the world's ways of doing things. And that was confusing to me, how he could have such integrity, without being a dried up old religious prune. He was clever, fun, and hopelessly sentimental. He was such an awesome man. And I couldn't believe that in my hand I was holding a personal video message from him. He was gone—dead and buried. Yet, he would speak to me again.

Was I ready to hear what he had to say?

The drive to Dad's office took eight minutes and 21 seconds—it should have taken at least 13. But I couldn't wait to pop in the DVD. Then again, I was scared to death. My heart was pumping faster than it did on my daily two-mile run.

Melissa had been tipped off regarding my arrival and met me at the door. *"Mike, how ARE you?"* she said, embracing me like a mother. She must have sensed the lump in my throat, and she rescued me by rattling on. *"You just go on in there and make yourself at home. I'm holding all calls, and I'll see to it that you're not disturbed for as long as you need to be there. Nancy and I will be here until 6—if you're still here, I'll have something brought in for you to eat. Just check my desk. Chinese okay for you?"*

I was amazed at the service I was given. Dad really knew how to pick his staff or train them. I actually managed to speak. *"Chinese would be great, Melissa, thanks."*

The door to Dad's office was open. I went on in. On Dad's desk was a steaming hot latte from Starbucks, a legal pad and pen. Melissa—and Dad—knew just what I needed. So when I saw the new box of Kleenex, I knew I was in for it.

I locked myself in and drew a deep breath. I wondered how many deep breaths Dad had taken in this room. This was his air; his office, where he breathed, worked and dreamed—and this was where he prayed. I heard him often. I used to play in here, I remembered. And even after so many prosperous years and remodelings by Mom, his office retained a quaintness that reflected the things he loved. He still had those aluminum toy semi-trucks we kids played with, now sitting on a handsome cherry-wood bookcase. Pictures of our family were everywhere, carefully framed. There was even a corkboard full of recent photos neatly arranged with pushpins. And there on his desk was the blobby clay turtle I made in third grade. It was no great piece of artwork, but it held a place of honor as chief paperweight in full view of all who entered. And on the wall, amid the plaques and photos and a beckoning seascape in oils, he still had that dated old big black poster on the wall with the names of Jesus in rainbow colors. He loved his Lord.

I sat in his big burgundy leather chair where he had wanted me to sit, and I felt swallowed up in it. I felt like a small, cheap imitation of my dad. Who was I, really? I knew I'd never be able to run his business. I got angry for a moment, but it drew tears out of my eyes. I was wimping out. I was wishing Dad hadn't found it so necessary to put me through this.

Then I became suddenly annoyed that I was questioning my own worth. Why should I be so hard on myself? I made myself remember that I had just earned an M.B.A. with a 4.0 GPA. And I was all set to pursue my Ph.D. in the fall. I was on an enviable track. The only reason I was going through with all this was because Dad went to the trouble of putting it all together, and because I was so anxious to hear his final words to me—not because I was entertaining the idea of becoming my father's successor. I thought I should just get all of this over with, so I could give Josh my unshakable NO and move on with my Ph.D. program.

I opened the thick padded envelope and found the letter and was warmed to see that it was penned in Dad's own hand.

> *Hello Son,*
>
> *If you're reading this, it means I've gone Home. I'm sorry for any pain and inconvenience that poses. Believe me, it wasn't planned!*
>
> *As I write to you, I know that my health is not as it should be. I'm under a doctor's care and all that, but I realize that at any moment I could suddenly be gone. And as I said, if you're reading this, I am. Don't worry—I died happy, and very confident of my destiny. To me, death is just the shedding of a cumbersome earth suit; I must certainly be dancing with Jesus as you read this! Believe me, I am enjoying the new digs.*
>
> *My heart-scare up North caused me to do a lot of thinking. I've tried to prepare you kids for life, both in this world and the world hereafter, but I'm not sure I've done it. And I hadn't made arrangements for the company, either. So this gift to you is two-fold. I am giving you headship over Montgomery Freight; but I'm also giving you instructions to ensure its success. I know that you're an educated man—perhaps by this time you've even earned that second degree you've been working on. But Son, there are some things this world just can't teach you about success.*
>
> *I've been trying to do the things I need to do to live as long as this takes to complete. I pray the Lord will allow me to finish it—I'm certainly doing my best to stick around awhile!*
>
> *I hope you will enjoy just one more long visit with your dad. This one is the most important of them all.*
>
> *I love you, Mike.*
>
> *Eternally yours,*
> *Dad*

The letter hit me like a ton of bricks, toppling what was left of my reserve—I couldn't stop the flood of tears that had stacked up behind my eyes. I remembered why I loved my dad so much. Since

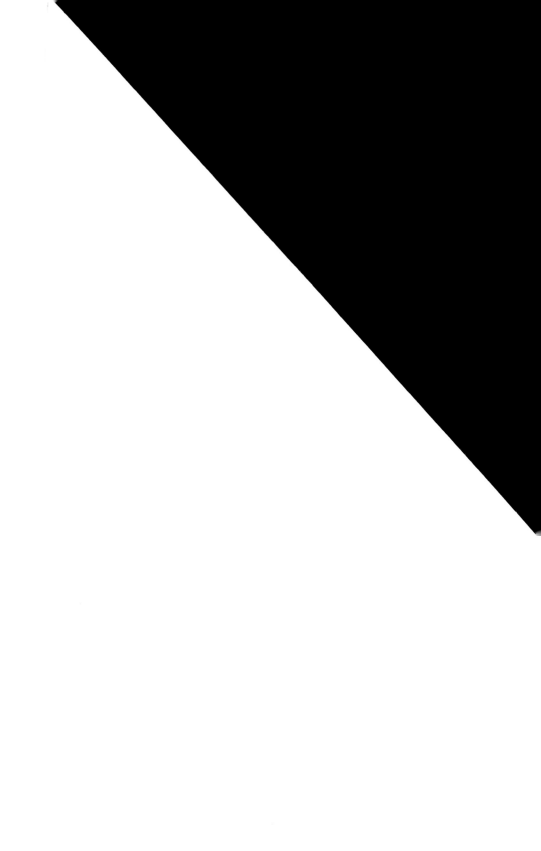

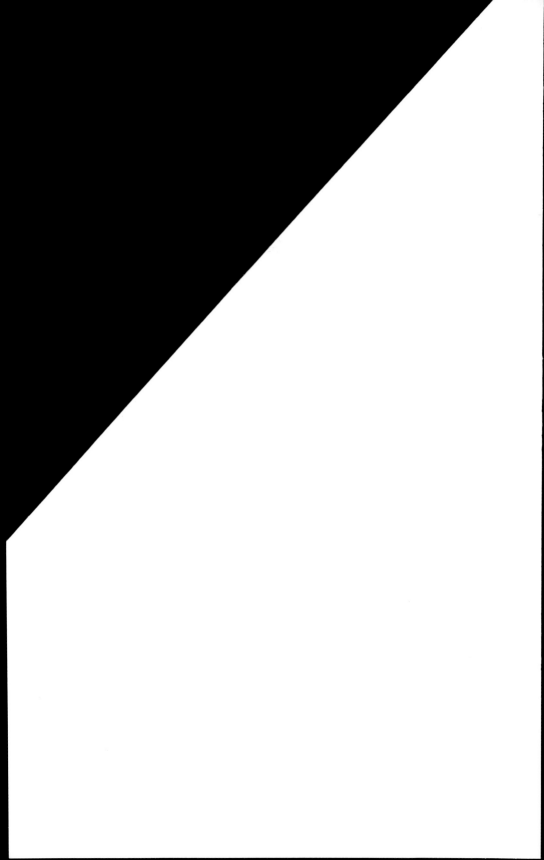

The Startling Gift of Preparation

Melissa had already booted up the computer, so I popped in the DVD.

I was amazed. This thing had music, graphics, the works. My swollen eyes began to fill again—Dad loved technology, and I could see he had solicited the help of the multimedia guy at church. He enjoyed creating this message. I felt good about that. A title faded in: The Plan of Your Life! And then he appeared on the screen—Dad, sitting in the chair that was now swallowing me up.

It all seemed so unreal. Dad seemed to look straight into my eyes as he spoke. *"Hello, Son. You look pretty good in my chair. How does it feel?"* Again, my head started spinning. I was shocked. There was Dad, as big as life. I hit the PAUSE button. He looked so good. Could this really be happening? I blinked back tears—I wanted to be able to see him, but the stupid tears…I swallowed hard and composed myself and hit the PLAY button again.

Mike, I've waited for years to see you sitting in my chair. You can't imagine how sorry I am that I will miss it. I guess you're all still shocked about this. Hope the family is O.K. I'm counting on you; always knew I could. All your life I told you the sky was the limit for you, and it is still true. I know your heart must be hurting. You probably feel clueless as to what the future holds for you, the family, and the business. And you might even be a little angry with me for saddling you with all this. Hang in there, Son, 'cause you are going to make it. You'll do more than survive. You will thrive. It may not look good today but I promise it will get better, and you will grow into the man you want to be.

As I watched him I saw that twinkle in his eye again—suppressing both smile and tear at once. *"What a privilege to be your dad!"* he said. I was so humbled to see such love for me! And he had some kind of strange faith in what I could be. I, on the other hand, felt overwhelmed. In no way was I capable of handling his company.

Son, what you're feeling is expected. I've been there. I know how you must feel.

I had to pause the video. He couldn't know how I feel! He had no idea how difficult this prospect would be for me—he didn't know how much I still felt like a kid.

Years ago, I was as you are—I was a grown man, but I still felt like a kid...

I laughed out loud, tears still blurring my eyes. I couldn't believe his timing, even post-mortem! I almost felt like Dad was watching this whole thing, and had thrown in the line just for comic relief. That would be so like him! The coincidental lift was healing somehow, and I managed to get beyond my loss to actually listen as he continued:

... But I got a big boost and break when I was close to your age. See, my pastor took me to lunch. It was a day I will never forget. He told me that he saw eagerness in me to learn, so he took me under his wing. He was a lifesaver—no, he was more than that. He was a life giver. He helped point me down a road that would help me become the man you know me to be. And while that man is not perfect by any stretch, he is a man who has been blessed of God beyond measure!

This pastor of mine asked me, 'Caleb, what are you planning to do with your life? It's obvious to me that God has His hand on you. You seem to me to have limitless potential.' I was really blown away by that—the fact that he saw limitless potential in me. But that's how I feel about you, Mike. Your potential is limitless. I know you have a hard time believing that. I was just like you. I didn't know WHO I was, so I was always working on WHAT I was. You're like that, too. You don't know your purpose. So you're afraid to fail. You're so afraid that you keep taking classes, hoping one of them will flip a switch in you and help you figure out who you want to be. Lots of folks do that—some do it by constantly changing jobs, starting new careers, coming up with new ideas that fizzle out before the rocket has even taken off. Now, it's always good to prepare yourself for the business world, and I'm so proud that you've been doing that. But you've got to hone Mike the person while you're crafting Mike the businessman. They have to be integrated in order to be successful and satisfied. And, Son, you can do it!

> Your potential is limitless.

> You don't know your purpose. So you're afraid to fail.

The pastor—he helped me by telling me I needed a plan. And he even helped me draft one. I'm going to do the same for you. Right here, right now.

> I needed a plan.

Wow! I had all this expertise at drawing up business plans and prospectuses, yet here was Dad, focusing on a plan for ME, Mike the grown man. I felt completely out of my element. But I trusted Dad. I watched and listened intently.

Remember the Fathead, life-sized poster you had of Peyton Manning in our den? As a freshman for the University of Tennessee, that boy was just a little ole third-string quarterback. But you'd never guess that. He showed up early and stayed late. In high school on weekends when his teammates were at the lake, Peyton was practicing with his receivers. He kept the same level of intensity at U.T. And it's a good thing. Because early in his first season, the first-string quarterback was injured. Now what are the odds that during the same game, the second-string quarterback would also be injured? But Peyton was prepared for the possibility. And when Coach Fulmer called Peyton's number, he was ready! For the next four years Peyton never came out of the huddle. But I can assure you, he never would have made it without a vision—a plan. Preparation and planning with a

He never would have made it without a vision— a plan. Preparation and planning with a purpose are essential for daily growth into your God-given potential.

purpose are essential for daily growth into your God-given potential. Remember, Son, hope—however noble—is not a strategy.

I know you didn't think this door would open so soon, if ever. And I guess, neither did I. We all think life here on earth lasts forever, but if you're watching this, you are painfully aware that it doesn't. After recovering from sudden heart failure in Rochester—and I'm so thankful for defibrillators and EMTs who know how to use them—I looked back on my life, and my effectiveness as a father. God has been gracious; he has taken up the slack, for sure! But I asked Him for more time. There was so much I was afraid I hadn't imparted to you, Candice and Zeke (yes, they're getting their own special messages!). I could have just taken you on a weekend retreat, but it wouldn't have the impact. This way, you can go back time after time and listen to your old man!

While I feel there's more to say to you, I don't feel in any way that I have failed! What a great son you are, Mike! You're so diligent in all you do! And you have a good heart. And whether you know it or not, you, like

God has been coaching your life.

Peyton Manning, have been in preparation for years—not just by getting an education. You see, God has been coaching your life. Your mother and I have prayed for His guidance over you since you were knee-high to a bird dog. As a result of His faithfulness, you are blessed in that you don't have to handle some of the baggage many of us had to haul. You've been prepared, even without realizing it. Remember how frustrated you would get at me for pushing you to be a person of scruples? I know you can recall rolling your eyes, thinking, "Not again, Dad!" Ha! But in spite of my boring delivery, you listened to part of it, anyway! And you're about to see all those past lessons pay off! The Holy Spirit will bring them to your remembrance, and they'll make sense now, because now you're desperate and humble. You're at a teachable place.

You have already seen so many miracles. Deep in your heart, you know what God can do. Look around, Son; this is the business God built. It seemed that as He grew me, the business grew with me. I've even heard you say that God has blessed me in this business. You believe! So ask God to help your areas of unbelief!

No matter how weak you feel, that little bit of faith is a great foundation. This plan will build on it. We'll start out with spiritual disciplines, physical disciplines and some financial goals. When my old pastor outlined this for me, I had no idea of where or how far the Lord would take me. I had no idea what doors He would open, what blessings He would bestow, not the least of which was my family. Every year I would polish my plan, going deeper and wider. I kept my family goals a high priority. For you to develop and maintain a personal growth plan will require faith and vision. Sadly, both are in short supply in our society and even in the church in America. You will need a strong faith to counterbalance all the problems you will face in this life. The Bible says faith is, "the assurance of things hoped for, the conviction of things not seen" (Hebrews 11:1). And faith is an absolute requirement if you want to please God—faith that we serve a big God who can do big things in and through our lives; faith that the future is bright; faith that God will come through; faith that with Him you can overcome mountains and break through barriers. If there is no faith for the future, there will be no power in the present. Faith keeps us going, growing and sowing. And you have to cultivate that faith! While we've all been given a measure to begin with,

> Faith keeps us going, growing and sowing.

it doesn't stay alive all by itself. And it certainly doesn't grow without a relationship with the Lord.

You are now a grown man with a purpose for yourself, for your family—or your future family if you're still single—and the Kingdom of God. This new career opportunity will serve you well if you follow the plan. And I know this will work. It worked for me. It sort of puts God's principles for success into a practical format.

Today's challenge is the very reason why I had you memorize verses like Jeremiah 29:11, "For I know the plans that I have for you, declares the Lord, plans for welfare and not for calamity to give you a future and a hope." You need to believe that your future is bright! God's got your back, Son, so get ready!

> You need to believe that your future is bright! God's got your back, Son, so get ready!

So this is kind of our final lap in our journey together. My prayer for you is that you will commit to grow into your full potential. It will require daily discipline and good decisions. It doesn't matter what everyone else does. What will YOU do? Great men aren't made

> It will require daily discipline and good decisions.

in a day—they are made daily. Pause the DVD for a minute, and dream of all God can do in you. He tells us in Ephesians 3:20 that He is, "able to do far more abundantly beyond all that we ask or think."

I did as he asked and paused the DVD. And I closed my eyes, squeezing out a tear. Could God really do for me the things Dad said He could? I did what Dad said, and I dreamed. I tried to see myself free of the constant fragmentation of my goals, the frustration it created, and the constant fear of messing up. Maybe it really was the lack of a plan that kept my life in constant chaos. And maybe Dad's faith-based plan could really work. Was that the key to Dad's strength,

> Maybe it really was the lack of a plan that kept my life in constant chaos.

his drive, his overall success? Could it work for me? I kept my eyes closed and just dreamed about that for a little bit…

I must have fallen asleep. I woke up drooling. Perhaps it was the faint aroma of lettuce wraps and General Tso's chicken. Yes, Melissa had gone home, and on her desk was a big bag of carryout from P.F. Chang's.

I grabbed the bag and headed back to my visit with Dad. I felt strangely peaceful—even hopeful. I wasn't afraid anymore. And I was ready to hear everything he had to say. I got back into the chair for the long haul and pushed PLAY again.

Build on a Solid Foundation

DAD CONTINUED:

So, Son, did you dream big? You should! You can have whatever you ask, when your motives are clean and free of selfishness and egotism. This contingency factor is found in James 4:3, "You ask and do not receive, because you ask with wrong motives, so that you may spend it on your pleasures." Keep your head on straight and you'll be fine.

I've outlined your "priority list." It sounds redundant that one can have more than one priority, since a priority implies foremost importance—and indeed your real priority is always to love God with all you are. That has to be your number one goal. And it's funny, but if you do that to the utmost degree, the other "priorities" will be met— just as Jesus said all commandments

> Your real priority is always to love God with all you are.

would be satisfied if we just loved the Lord with all we are and love others with the same consideration we have for ourselves. But I'm going to give you four other "priorities." They're really just part of the first, but it might help to see it broken down into doable parts. These things need to take precedence over other things in your life. Each of these areas has to work together in order to work at all! You really can't have one without the other. Let's take a look at Priority One:

Priority #1—Your Spiritual Life and Foundation. You are to, "... love the Lord your God with all your soul, body, mind and spirit" (Deuteronomy 6:5, paraphrased). This is the most important verse in the Old Testament. In the New Testament, Jesus affirmed it to be the number one command in the entire Bible. This issue is not to be taken lightly.

As you know Son, I love the Lord and He has been my anchor, the foundation for my life, business and our family. Many people choose different things to be their center, their anchor, their focus; I chose God, or maybe He chose me. But centering your life on Christ is the most important building block I want to pass on to you. I wish there were a way for me to emphasize how critical this issue really is. Perhaps the reality will unfold with the plan.

Over the years at our company, I have watched many families fragment, lives disintegrate, fortunes collapse. I've seen people endure untold problems and pain. And every life that crashed on the rocks with the sweeping tide was one lacking a strong foundation. This is the key for you not to just survive in life but

> I am talking about your foundation— what you choose to build your life and your forever on.

to thrive, even when others fail. I am talking about your foundation—what you choose to build your life and your forever on.

Many people think faith to be a secondary issue at best; others feel it's not even important for success at all. But Jesus said, "What does it profit a man to gain the whole world and lose his own soul?" (Mark 8:36, paraphrased). A great question too few query or contemplate. You can achieve great things in life, but without God what do you have, especially when it's all over? I have seen many climb the ladder to great success and wealth, yet as many arrive at the top they realize how empty life is without a foundation. I have heard it said, "Life here on earth is heaven practice." I believe it!

Let me share a parable with you that Jesus shared with His disciples; it is found in Luke 6:46-49:

> *"Why do you call Me, 'Lord, Lord,' and do not do what I say? Everyone who comes to Me and hears My words and acts on them, I will show you whom he is like: he is like a man building a house who dug deep and laid a foundation on the rock and when a flood occurred, the torrent burst against that house and could not shake it; because it had been well built. But the one who has heard and has not acted accordingly, is like a man who built a house on the ground without any foundation; and the torrent burst against it and immediately it collapsed, and the ruin of that house was great."*

What more important issue can you consider than what you will build your life upon?

The "house" that Jesus was talking about was not a physical building, but a life. He was talking about our lives, your life. What more important issue can you consider than what you will build your life upon? Notice, Jesus is crystal clear that we are to act upon His words. Today, people look at the Bible as a book to study, memorize, debate, even disbelieve. But it is really a book of action! We really only believe the parts of the Bible we do—the doing is the evidence that we believe. It's the "works" part of faith. Without it, faith is dead, having no expression. Jesus said that a person who "comes to Me and hears My words and acts on them" is a person with a good foundation. So, do you have a good foundation? What are you acting upon? Many people never even think at this level, so lives end up being built by default instead of a design and deliberate decision. Today, make your decision as to

We really only believe the parts of the Bible we do.

what you will build your life upon. I trust you will make the right call.

In the parable we see that circumstances turned badly for both men in the story. Storms, winds, and floods blasted their "houses"—their lives— and yet one stood and could not be destroyed because of the firmness

Many people never even think at this level, so lives end up being built by default instead of a design and deliberate decision.

of the foundation. I can make the same promise to you that Jesus made to all His followers in John 16:33, "In the world you have tribulation." I have certainly experienced it, and so has everyone I have ever known; problems, trials, stuff just happens. You have to be ready! Being ready has a lot to do with your foundation; what your life is built upon. Jesus went on to say, "But take courage; I have overcome the world." He is the foundation that will hold up when all hell breaks loose! Will you be able to

Will you be able to stand strong in the storms?

stand strong in the storms? You will, if the precepts of Christ are what your life is built upon!

Jesus' warning about the lack of foundation was clear. He said the man who built his house on the ground without a solid foundation was in effect asking for disaster—even unknowingly planning for it. Without a foundation, a house will be swept away when floodwaters sweep in. The same happens to a house with a faulty foundation. The house slips away, turns over and falls apart, becoming a mess of debris in rushing waters. This is what happens to people who live their lives by happenstance—let-

It's the most important issue of every person's life.

ting life just happen without making plans for a secure foundation. It's the most important issue of every person's life. So you, Son, must choose your foundation; you must decide what you will build your life on. And you cannot delay—storms can come without warning.

Look out the window at that big oak tree. The roots of that tree go much deeper than the little flowering pear across the street. The biggest trees have the deepest roots. And the tallest—and safest—buildings have the deepest foundations. A single-story ranch home might have a shallow, 2-ft. foundation. But the foundation of the Empire State building runs 55 ft. deep! More depth is required to anchor the height. By the same token, the higher you want to go in life, the deeper you must dig your spiritual foundation. I know that you have never wanted your life to be ordinary. You want your life to count for something—not just to succeed for yourself, but I know you have a heart to help others be successful as well. And I know you want a family someday. You want a marriage that will last. And you'll want those kids to look up to you

> The higher you want to go in life, the deeper you must dig your spiritual foundation.

for help with the tough issues. If you really want this, you must build on something solid and immovable, or what you build in life will topple over. Jesus said he was going to build His church on a Rock, not on a sandy beach or shifting soil. He also said that the wise man builds his house on the rock. A solid foundation is a common theme throughout the Bible. God wants you to dig deep and build on the Rock. The Rock of which the Scriptures speak is Jesus. You can build your life on Him and His Word and you will never be sorry. I've never met anyone that regretted living for Jesus and trying to live the Bible, but I've met many who regretted NOT living for Jesus. It's never too late to begin.

> It's never too late to begin.

Your foundation can be loosely recognized as what you revolve your life around. The earth revolves around the sun, its source of light. What is at the center of your life? Throughout Scripture we are encouraged to build on the Rock—Jesus, the Word. I have found all other foundations to be as perilous as quicksand for a man, his family and his business.

Son, many people I know say they love, or at least know God. Now, I cannot be anyone's judge, but I never have understood why so many of these Christ-followers don't develop a plan to go deeper, nearer, closer with God. Too many of them just call upon the Lord when there's a problem. Having no deep foundation, one major life problem can cause a domino effect of devastation. Finances bottom out. The wife gets frustrated. The kids become irritations. Soon it's all chaos. But if you are going to be the man God wants you to be, you must let God be foundational to all you are. Let Him in on every issue you face. "In all your ways acknowledge Him and He will make your paths straight" (Proverbs 3:6). Romans 8:28 says: "...God causes all things to work together for good to those who love God..." God knows and sees the whole "movie" of your life at once, while you're only seeing one frame at a time. I'm talking about a lifetime commitment, not a single event. As my friend, John Maxwell taught me, "Disciples are made daily, not in a day." Keep as a focus your plan, progress and relationship with Jesus. Jude 20 commands and commissions us, "...building yourselves up on your most holy faith..." Digging a foundation is not easy, but the effort will always pay off—just look around you.

> I never have understood why so many of these Christ-followers don't develop a plan to go deeper, nearer, closer with God.

> Digging a foundation is not easy, but the effort will always pay off—just look around you.

I'm sure you remember all the building and renovation projects we did while you lived at home. You called me a "slave-driver" on many occasions! I'm sure I must have seemed like one. But it was all that work that helped you develop your great work ethic you have today. Many of the projects we took on were a lot harder than we first imagined. I guess they all were, come to think of it! Any time anyone chooses to upgrade or renovate a room, yard, or any project, it usually takes longer, costs more and makes a bigger mess than was planned for. I guess that is one of the reasons most people take a pass on a life of constant change and growth. It is so sad. Without question, there is pain in change, but the final product is worth the effort that's put into the project.

There is pain in change.

Remember when we poured the driveway at the lake house we built? What a job! Pouring concrete is always a beast. First, we had to make sure we had the forms deep enough that the concrete would stand up to the traffic and the weight that would be on it. Next, we had to make sure we had put enough steel in before we poured the slab so it would be strong enough to stand up for years. Without the steel, the driveway would crack under the weight of a car or truck. Not very attractive. Not very useful, either. Who wants to scrape their undercarriage on a craggy, bumpy slab of broken concrete?

Finally we had to pick the strength of the concrete the company would deliver. The weaker the mix of the concrete, the cheaper the product; cutting costs here was not an option if we wanted the driveway to last. It is the same with the foundation you are building your life upon. Don't skimp or you'll pay the price!

Don't skimp or you'll pay the price!

Family problems and destruction always begin with a crack. Don't wait for cracks to appear and then try to fill them—that's being reactive and not proactive. Build it right the first time. If you miss this point, God will be there with a remedy, but it might be a very bitter pill.

Make faith your foundation. Sounds religious, but it's really very practical. And it's essential. Your foundation must be dependent on Jesus Christ. This is a different mindset than the do-it-yourself, independent, self-seeking attitude of today's marketplace. But dependence on Christ is like building your house on that Rock. It starts with faith: "And without faith it is impossible to please Him, because anyone who comes to God must believe that He is and that He is a rewarder of those who seek Him" (Hebrews 11:6).

A foundation of faith is made up of building blocks—and of course, Jesus is the cornerstone. These blocks will help you put it all together. Look at the form I created for your spiritual growth plan in the envelope. [See the Appendix in the back of this book] There I've listed building blocks, important spiritual disciplines you must develop and deploy daily in order to keep your faith strong.

> Important spiritual disciplines you must develop and deploy daily in order to keep your faith strong.

These are the Building Blocks of a Spiritual Foundation:

- Bible Reading

- Bible Study

- Scripture Memory

- Meditation

- Silence

- Solitude

- Prayer

- Fasting

- Evangelism

- Books

- CDs, DVDs, Podcasts and Blogs

- Service

- Mission Trips

Quantify each discipline, daily, weekly, monthly, or annually. That means, set up a schedule for yourself and stick to it. This begins your formation of a transformational growth plan. If you don't list, don't quantify and don't keep up with your progress, you likely will not accomplish much. It's like keeping up with your bankbook or check register. If you try to guess how much money is in there, you'll almost always overestimate! Likewise, we usually think we do more than we do to cultivate a spiritual life. The time we think we spend communing with Christ is usually less than the reality. So if your faith is to be a priority, you must plan and make it a priority!

> We usually think we do more than we do to cultivate a spiritual life.

This might feel like work at first, but it's really simply a matter of positioning. You're moving yourself into a place where you can be transformed by the renewing of your mind. A couple of chapters of Bible reading might not seem like it's doing much for you. But a daily regimen of it actually begins to change a person's thinking patterns and enlivens the spirit. It positions you to hear spiritually. You don't have to even think about change—it will happen! Does a caterpillar work hard to develop those awesome butterfly wings? No way. Its only work is in building the cocoon according to God's design. Then it simply yields to the miracle of metamorphosis. In that cocoon, it rests in the hands of

> This might feel like work at first, but it's really simply a matter of positioning.

> Then it simply yields to the miracle of metamorphosis.

its Creator, and wakes up a butterfly. That little worm will spend the rest of its life flying around and looking good. We who are of the family of faith also work with the miracle of metamorphosis. Romans 12:2 reads, "And do not be conformed to this world, but be transformed by the renewing of your mind..." The word used in the command to be "transformed" is the same word from which we get our word metamorphosis. If we will commit to a life of faith and growth, God will daily transform us. He will "metamorph-us" into something awesome. It is a process and not an event. It is a lifelong commitment to become all God desires for you to be. If you saw the movie "Transformers," that is what we should be called as we continue to grow—not machines, but transformed! It will only happen if you make a choice to make it happen as a priority in your life. Think of it as your personal software program: U-2.0—the upgrade! A new you!

> He will "metamorph-us" into something awesome.

> Think of it as your personal software program: U-2.0 —the upgrade! A new you!

Those building blocks I've listed are designed to help you build that cocoon. They're all Bible-based, and they're all essential elements as you build the foundation of your life. Everything else depends on this foundation—your family, your business, your personal satisfaction in life.

Now, let's break some of the blocks down to see what they're really made of. Each area—Bible Study, Meditation, Fasting, etc.—must be integrated into your life. It's got to become part of your existence... your spiritual DNA. It may seem like work at first, but believe me, it's more work to neglect these foundational building blocks and to end up building a rickety spiritual existence. Just think about each area and write down how you can address it

> Your spiritual DNA.

in your daily life. I call this a Personal Growth Plan. Let me show you an example.

Here's my own Personal Growth Plan for a given year:

- Have two hours of devotional time, five days per week

- Memorize 52 Bible verses

- Read Old Testament through once

- Read New Testament through twice

- Spend time meditating on the Bible five days per week

- Read 52 books in addition to Bible readings

- Fast 12 days out of the year

- Share my faith with 26 people

- Have a two-day personal prayer retreat

Now, remember, that's MY Personal Growth Plan. You don't have to read 52 additional books, or fast for 12 days, for example. You might choose to read three books and fast 30 days. It's all very personal. I like reading, and feel that it broadens me as a thinker and that it enlightens me as a soul winner. I love my little prayer retreats, but you may choose to meet alone with God for two weeks instead of two days. My point is not to set your goals, but to inspire them.

> My point is not to set your goals, but to inspire them.

In addition to the above list, I have some other goals for myself—goals relating to my individual interests, weaknesses, abilities and family needs. I call this section simply, "Other Areas of Improvement." Let me show you how this works by listing my own personal target areas and goals to improve upon this year:

- Public Speaking (church conferences and businessmen's meetings)

- Networking (with other businesses and with new people in church)

- Budgeting

- Writing (yes, I still hope to do that book someday!)

- Personal exercise—30 minutes, five days per week

- Weight—Maintain 180 lbs.

- Disciple my kids

- Have a date night each week with my wife

- Have family dinner together once per week

- Spend time with my son-in-law

- Be debt free

Again, this list is completely subjective and individualized. One of your goals might be to join a church home group or go cycling once a week, Could Jesus be interested in such things? Absolutely! After all, it's God who richly provides us with every-thing for our enjoyment (1 Timothy 6:17). He's into anything that will enrich your life, health, relationships, character or sense of well-being. Son, if I've ever spoken truth to you, this is it. If you get only one thing out of our time together, get this point! [See the Appendix for worksheets]

I pushed the PAUSE button again to study that Personal Growth Plan a bit more carefully. Wow! Dad was doing ALL those things? I looked at my life. What was I doing every day? I had no devotional life to speak of…I hadn't spoken to God in a long time. I was just going through my days as if they'd never end. I woke up, grabbed a donut or some-thing, ran a mile or so, went to classes, ate, went to work, went out with friends, came home, fooled around on Facebook, did home-work and went to bed. That was my life. I just took it as it came. Every day was unstructured, and for the most part, unproductive. And I wondered why I always felt like a big goof.

My life had no plan. I had been living a reactive life instead of a proactive one. I wasn't in charge of my life enough to even give it to God! I just let life happen to me, and when

> My life had no plan.

I was up against a wall, I reacted and tried to fix it.

Dad wasn't passive like that. His only passivity was in yielding his human will to the higher will of the Lord. That submission was his hidden strength. It gave him the Plan—and the same principles were being imparted to me.

> That submission was his hidden strength. It gave him the Plan.

I felt as though God were speaking directly into my life. And I suppose He was.

Your Family Can Help You Fly

DAD CONTINUED:

As I'm filming this, you're still a young, unmarried man. But I hope you do find a mate and come to enjoy the blessings of fatherhood! It's made my own life so rich! So I admonish you, when you do find the right woman, do not enter into that marriage covenant lightly! I pray you will never experience an unhappy marriage, and I hope that divorce to you will never be an option. While a problem home will create an unhappy life, a broken covenant will bring the sorrow to a much deeper level, with ramifications you cannot even imagine. I have watched this far too often.

Trust me here; please make commitment to family a priority in your planning and daily life. Most leave this area to chance, like the roll of the dice; and they usually come up "snake eyes."

> Most leave this area to chance, like the roll of the dice; and they usually come up "snake eyes."

I know your breakup with Allison was beyond painful. But things may have been worse if she hadn't cancelled the wedding. You see, after the excitement and newness of being married wears off, so does the ability to keep minor irritations from showing. With time, familiarity erodes your reserve; you begin to voice what you really think and feel. This brings a whole new dimension of our personalities to the fore—and both parties have to get to know these new "persons." They don't always seem compatible. But addressing the issues with the sensitivity and openness of Christ will enable incompatible aspects of personality to become compatible! This process is part of becoming one—but it's not always easy. That's why it is vital that you know how to take conflict before the Lord, and that you choose a mate who shares that ability to work things out God's way. After the wedding and

> But addressing the issues with the sensitivity and openness of Christ will enable incompatible aspects of personality to become compatible!

the initial excitement of sharing daily life, you have to deal with the realities of differing opinions, habits, irritations and pet peeves. You and Allison had your share of differences, even without living together. So for the time being, you might do well to thank the Lord for your present situation and adopt the motto, "I'd rather be single than wish I was!" Or, "I'd rather want what I don't have, than have what I don't want!" King Solomon said that, "It is better to live in a desert than with a quarrelsome and ill-tempered wife" (Proverbs 21:19, paraphrased). So being single isn't necessarily the worst thing that could happen to a man!

Choose your mate with care. This life plan can help. The more your mate can identify with your life plan, the more compatible you will be in every life area. There will always be more to do than you will have time for; that is why you must choose wisely how you spend every second you have. We all have 86,000 seconds in a day; choose wisely how you spend the seconds. Justice Charles Dow Richards once said, "Don't be

> "Don't be fooled by the calendar. There are only as many days in the year as we make use of. One person gets a week's value out of a year while another person gets a year's value out of a week."

fooled by the calendar. There are only as many days in the year as we make use of. One person gets a week's value out of a year while another person gets a year's value out of a week."

Let your plan and priorities answer the issue of the calendar. Live by the words of Ephesians 5:16 which supports good planning, "…making the most of your time, because the days are evil."

There is a famous scene in the original Peter Pan movie that goes something like this. Peter is in the children's bedroom and they want to know how to fly like he does. They try jumping from the floor and even from the beds without liftoff. They become frustrated. "How do you do it?" John asks and Peter points out the key: "You need to think happy thoughts!" In the remake of the original movie (called Hook), Peter is a grown man, far from Neverland and has long been domesticated. His children are in Neverland and in danger; he has to go back to rescue them. He tries to fly, again without liftoff—until he thinks of his family. That was his happy thought! And away he flies! Does your family help your liftoff? Son, you guys were always my happy thought—and you gave me wings to soar. It is my prayer you have the same experience in life. But it will require work and a plan.

Priority #2—Your Family. It is my hope that as you reflect on our family over the years you can see how important you guys were to me. Obviously, Mom has been the Queen of the Castle. It is so awesome how great life can be if you marry well! Your mom made our lives great. So like I said, choose wisely.

Your wife will need attention, and so will your children. I've tried to "be there" for you three kids. Football and rugby games were always on my schedule, always a priority. Both of you boys were such good athletes, and that made sitting in the stands and hearing the people talk about you and your brother even more fun. I was frequently overcome with pride! Remember when you sacked the quarterback against the state champions on the last play, and we won? They talked about you on the radio during the post-game highlights. I couldn't help crying as we drove home. Yes, I thank God daily for you guys.

But whether your kids are football stars, whether they excel in anything at all, they will need you. They will need your affirmation. But more, they will need your presence. All kids have exhibits in the school fair, so make their school fairs a priority. Go and see their little school papers hanging in the hall. Gush over them—you shouldn't have to force it! Be proud of every accomplishment they make in school, however small. Reschedule dinners with clients—they can wait. Your children must know that they are more important than any business deal.

> Your children must know that they are more important than any business deal.

Here at the company, I have watched many people succeed in business and receive promotion after promotion. You would think they would all be happy, but not all were. As I've been able to see it, a major difference between the ones who enjoyed life and the ones who didn't, had to do with the family they had cultivated. Whatever they went home to every evening made the difference in how they experienced life. I have learned it is not financial or professional success that makes life worth living, but the people you love the most. Few would debate this point, yet how many do you know have a plan to improve their family life? You can come home to heaven or hell. And divorce does not have to be the solution. Again, be proactive, not reactive. Cultivate a good marriage; grow a loving family, like a garden. It's your choice.

> You can come home to heaven or hell.

> Cultivate a good marriage; grow a loving family, like a garden. It's your choice.

In our culture people try to divide their lives into different compartments and focus on each one individually. You can't do it with your family because it, like faith, affects every aspect of your life. That is why this section is vital to your future.

If you read the book of Genesis, you will see the first institution God created was the family. It was instituted before the Church, any government, or school. It was number one because it was designed by the Master Architect as the primary building block for society and life.

Jesus said, "... Any Kingdom divided against itself is laid waste; and any city or house divided against itself will not stand" (Matthew 12:25). That includes your family. If it is divided it will not stand the storms that will come. So, Son, it is critical that you develop and deploy a plan to grow your family. Mother Teresa was asked, upon receiving the Nobel Peace Prize, "What can we do to promote world peace?" She said, "If you want to promote world peace, go home and love your family." Wise words from a lady committed to helping others.

Let me give you six important qualities you will need to build a rock solid family. The list is not exhaustive, but will give you a great place to start.

Six Qualities to Build a Rock Solid Family

I.   An Unwavering Commitment

Strong families have a sense of being a team. When you were younger we called ourselves "Team Montgomery!" It was one thought that helped us accomplish so much as a family. We were committed to one another. To be divided for any reason was unthinkable. Today, culture has made family commitment an option, not an absolute. Rather than be determined to work through issues and change, we're encouraged to leave painful situations and seek happiness elsewhere. To do so presents a grievous paradox.

Parents go their separate ways seeking happiness, and the kids in the middle only find devastation. As Margaret Thatcher, former Prime Minister of Great Britain said, "Standing in the middle of the road is very dangerous; you get knocked down by the traffic from both sides." I came from a broken home and know first-hand that this is true. Never let your children experience such unspeakable internal conflict. Plan ahead. Choose a wife with whom you can honestly com-

> "Standing in the middle of the road is very dangerous; you get knocked down by the traffic from both sides."

municate—one who chooses to place her own life upon Christ the solid Rock. With Christ as your foundation, you can work through anything. And remember that commitment is a decision.

II. Spend Plenty of Time Together

If you asked a biblical scholar what is the most important verse in the Old Testament, they would respond that it is the Shama. Deuteronomy 6:4-7: "Hear, O Israel! The LORD is our God, the LORD is one! You shall love the LORD your God with all your heart and with all your soul and with all your might. These words, which I am commanding you today, shall be on your heart. You shall teach them diligently to your sons and shall talk of them when you sit in your house and when you walk by the way and when you lie down and when you rise up." In this very important and ancient command, God gives us four great times for family:

"Sit in your house." This would be mealtime. This is imperative for many reasons, one being that kids who eat meals with their family make better grades. Capitalize on this time. Do not watch TV or look at the computer screen while eating, but have dialogue with the most important people in your life. Part of your plan needs to include this time.

"Walk by the way." Very few of us walk anywhere these days, so let's substitute travel time. If you added up how much time you spend in the car, it's astronomical; check your gasoline receipts if you doubt me. Travel time is a great time for the kids or for the whole family. Don't be tempted to stick in a DVD to keep the kids occupied so they don't drive you crazy as you drive. Plan instead for drive time discussions, games, devotions, or other family-building opportunities.

"When you lie down." Bedtime is a great family time. Games, prayers, talks—the sky is the limit if you have a plan. Then after the kids go to bed you and your spouse can have your own special family time—another super reason for an early bedtime for the kids.

"When you rise up." The morning is a great family time that almost everyone misses today. The reason we blow this opportunity is that most Americans are allergic to the morning! This virtual allergy to getting up creates conflict in the home that does not promote family and a positive atmosphere. Again, at the risk of redundancy, you must plan for this time. It is the best part of the day,

> Most Americans are allergic to the morning.

and part of your preparation must be going to bed at a decent hour. Just a thought. For most of your life you kids were like vampires, up late at night, sleeping through the morning. But if I could go back, I would set you kids on a different schedule, and we would enjoy our mornings together before work and school took us our separate ways.

Here is a list of some ways you can make the above points practical:

Date Your Mate—There will always be something to threaten the follow-through on this one, always an interruption, a preemptive event, another person in need of your listening ear. But nothing is more romantic to a woman than being a priority. Take your wife out to dinner, and follow it with a drive out to a lake at sunset, or just take a stroll in the park, holding hands. You need that time as much as she, and it will do wonders for your relationship. Gentleness will descend upon you both, and your days will carry a longing to do it again—to really connect in spirit.

Have Family Devotions—This is more important than I can say. I regret that I waited so long to institute devotional time into our family life. By the time I realized its importance, you and Candice were older and other things were always beckoning you from the family circle. It's hard to compete with television and phone calls to friends. But Zeke was younger and was able to form the habit. To this day, he enjoys devotional times with your mom and me. We have great conversations, and really get to the heart of issues this way. Talking about God's Word together enables us to open our hearts—to know, and to be known. It is a vital part of real communication. And it provides an assurance that your family is being exposed to the Word of God on a daily basis.

> Talking about God's Word together enables us to open our hearts—to know, and to be known.

Develop Family Hobbies—Hobbies are a great way to connect as a family. I suppose sports can be called a hobby—and I'm so glad you kids enjoyed them as much as I! What fun we had as a family, going to ball games and watching Candice at her swim meets! Even watching football together—those were some of our best times! You like fishing. Perhaps your wife and children will take interest in it as well, and you can learn about lures, poles, and the habits of fish; and where they're apt to be when you go looking for them. The Porters enjoy gardening together as a family, and the Flynns play music. Some families collect things and go hunting antiques together to add to their collections. Hobbies are as diverse as people. But when you can get a family interested in one thing—wow! What fun!

Disciple Your Kids (or grandkids)—Remember our weekly breakfast while you were in high school? It was a cherished time for me, even if you were half asleep! I did it for all three of you—breakfast and a brief devotional discussion and accountability on the way to school. God used our devotional commitment to help make you who you are today—not what you are. You may not like what you are at this moment. But that is going to change! You are a work in progress and, I believe, a man "after God's own heart." Employ this plan and watch your life transform!

> Employ this plan and watch your life transform!

Family Dinner Together—The younger your children are, the more time is required at home in the evenings. You can let their life stage help determine your family calendar. But as they grow older, there will be football practice, soccer practice, choir practice, dance team practice, gymnastics meets, science club, Spanish club, debate team…whatever your children are drawn to in the way of extracurriculars will make family mealtime a challenge. You will have to let them go at times. But do not let the interruptions cause you to eliminate family dinnertime altogether. Your son may say he grabbed a sandwich at 4:00; your daughter will claim that she's not hungry, or is working on an important paper for school. My advice: Regardless of who's not hungry, make a point of assembling together at the family table. Food isn't the issue as much as the fellowship and conversation. Try to keep family dinnertime intact.

Take Vacations—Remember, while you have time with your family on earth—BE THERE! Make the most of the time God gives you! Set aside uninterruptible time to be together as a family—at a fun place; an interesting place; a place to build relationships, enjoy one another and build memories. There is so much more I would love to have done with you guys—camping, boating, motorcycle rides, cruises, movies… Learn off my dime, because time passes quickly (I was sure I would still be with you at this point of life). Prioritize, or someone else will do it for you. The Bible says, "Your life is like a vapor, here today and gone tomorrow" (James 4:14, paraphrased). Even though I prepared this whole deal for you to take over (you know, just in case), I really thought I would still be there today. Trust me, Son, time flies. So make every moment count.

> Prioritize, or someone else will do it for you.

The pain in my dad's face was palpable as he said these words. The thought of leaving us was as difficult as what I was feeling.

Son, I was never more keenly aware of this than when I walked your sister down the aisle and "gave her away!" Those three words now have a far more serious ring to them. As the doors opened, the aisle looked a mile long. And why was the groom smiling so broadly? As a part of the service the pastor had all four parents

> Gave her away!

stand up. He looked right at me and asked if I realized I was giving up all rights and responsibilities for my baby girl. She would now assume a new last name and be gone. It was at that instant that I actually had "second thoughts." Would he care for her, love her and help her grow? I wondered if I had done enough, spent enough time, and mentored her enough. It was too late to wonder. Before I knew it they were off on a cruise. Please prioritize and plan the things most important in the world. I'm not sure if I showed it or not, but you, Son, and our family were more important than any of you ever realized. In the envelope there is a worksheet I developed for you to use in the process of your plan. (See Appendix p. 157)

III. An Attitude of Gratitude for Each Other

Strong families not only love each other; they are unbelievably grateful to be on the same team. This doesn't just happen without some serious work on the part of the family members. This requires a plan on your part, Son. Our nature is to be negative and look for the bad qualities in our family members. It's hard to be grateful if your focus is negative. And it requires a plan to be positive. Part of my devotional routine was to thank God for your mom and you three kids; it caused me to stop and take note of the amazing qualities placed in you by God—qualities He wanted me to help bring out. You kids were His, and it was my job to prepare you to serve Him with all that is within you. I never tried to protect you from the church, but I tried to prepare you for the church.

> You kids were His, and it was my job to prepare you to serve Him with all that is within you.

IV. Constant and Clear Communication

Communication requires that we put our family members first. In your communication, if you seek to understand before you seek to be understood, life will be much better. Most people just want to share their thoughts without getting the other person's ideas. But the Bible records, "...be quick to hear, slow to speak..." (James 1:19). Balancing what you hear and speak will require constant monitoring, or you will miss important messages. Not getting what your family is trying to say is a real problem. I learned a great communication trick with your mom early in our marriage. When she made a comment that made me mad, I would ask: "This is what I just heard you say; but what did you mean?" Communication without caution creates easy access for the devil. Head him off at the pass!

> If you seek to understand before you seek to be understood, life will be much better.

V. The Ability to Triumph in Tribulations

Every family on planet Earth will experience problems. This is a universal problem of mankind. The issue is not that we will have problems; but how we will handle the problems that arise. Part of your plan must be the ability to cope in contrary circumstances. When I was a kid, there was a lot of yelling in my home, so that is how I learned to deal with issues—by yelling. That is until I married your mom. She grew up in a home where she never once saw her parents argue or yell. And as a result, she was as cool as a cucumber, even in adversity. As you can imagine, this caused certain strains in the relationship. I had to learn to express my intensity without yelling! Not an easy task, and I never got full victory. That point I made a while ago about familiarity eroding your reserve, causing you to express what you think and feel—it applies here. See, I have come to know about this experientially! Early in our marriage, some minor thing would irritate me, and I would express myself in the way I had learned at home, I suppose. Your mother would sense the caustic edge to my remark and interpret it in light of her peaceful home background, get this teary-eyed look on her face and gently say, "You're yelling at me." I would think, "Girl, you have no idea what real yelling sounds like!" But I had to learn to preserve peace, to communicate with understanding. Temperance in this area was a hard lesson for me. I am grateful for the grace and patience of your mother.

VI. Spiritual Health

You have heard me say many times that a family that prays together stays together. It's true. There is something so precious about a family yielding together before the Lord. Even Dad is subject to the Lord God Almighty! It's important for kids to see that. It's also important for kids to learn to speak to the Lord openly. Some families are

> A family that prays together stays together.

embarrassed to share such intimacy. And prayer *is* intimate. But if you start a pattern of prayer from the day you're married, you will enhance your union together and with God in ways you cannot imagine. You remember what I told you in our faith section: it is of primary importance. I love what Joshua said as he neared his death: "...as for me and my house, we will serve the Lord" (Joshua 24:15). It was his declaration of faith for himself and his family. I would challenge you to make it yours. It doesn't matter what any other family does. What will you do? Make your plan and work it, and I promise, you will be glad for it.

Former President George H. W. Bush was asked, *"What is your greatest accomplishment in life?"* He could have replied that as a fighter pilot in WWII, he was shot down and survived; or that he was U.S. Ambassador to China, or was Vice President of the United States, or that he was the President, or won the victory in the Persian Gulf War with few casualties, or had two sons as state governors and one a two-term President. Yet Bush said, *"My children still come home."* That is an accomplishment, indeed.

As Dad wrapped up the point, I noticed I'd been taking copious notes—I was back in school after all! But something was telling me that I was about to earn something much more **I was getting a life.** valuable than a couple more letters behind my name. I was getting a life.

Your Bod from God

By this time, I was on the office couch, watching Dad with my feet propped up and taking notes on my iPad. I was enjoying my time with him. I was done with the lettuce wraps and chicken, and had a real hankering for some chocolate pie or something…then Dad's next chapter heading appeared:

Priority #3—Your Physical Body. I noticed the iPad was sitting on MY pad of extra girth . . . it wasn't much, but enough to feel just a little bit conspicuous before the topic at hand. I remembered Dad, how in recent years—months, especially—had come to adopt a much stricter lifestyle of fitness. And he seemed so physically fit for his age. He shouldn't have died! I thought to myself.

I remembered what Dad had said in the letter: "I've been trying to do the things I need to do to live as long as this takes to complete. I pray the Lord will allow me to finish it—I'm certainly doing my best to stick around awhile!" I was glad that he did finish it. And it inspired me to do whatever I needed to do to fulfill my own tasks on earth. Suddenly the chocolate pie didn't seem that important. I hit the remote and settled in to hear more from the man I love more than any other.

DAD CONTINUED:

Well, Son, it should go without saying, but let me anyway. On earth you will only get one body. I'm sure I like my new body in heaven better than the one I had there. But it just might be that I could have spent a bit more time in that old body and lived to see the rest of my grandchildren had I taken better care of my earth suit. You're young now, and even still on the athletic side, and today this probably doesn't seem important, but it will! I promise! Remember when you graduated from high school, and I asked you to lose about 50 lbs. of football weight? When I was young I never thought about weight or being in shape. Later though, I had no choice, and neither will you. The older I got, the more exercise and diet became a must. I needed energy and stamina for all I wanted to do. If I was going to accomplish all God desired for me, I had to stay in shape. Start earlier and it will be easier. A friend of mine named David told me it isn't fair for people to neglect their health, and then when they get old and sickly, to be a burden on their kids. Sometimes this cannot be avoided, but other times people choose to neglect their physical fitness and someone else has to pay for it in many ways.

It is so important you take care of yourself in this area. You have always been healthy and strong, but do not leave your health to chance. Let me put a spiritual spin on this situation. When you gave your heart to Jesus, you gave your whole self to Him. That means He owns you: lock, stock, and barrel; tax, title, and license. That includes your physical body. He expects and even commands that you take care of it for Him.

> When you gave your heart to Jesus, you gave your whole self to Him.

This is what He said; "But the one who joins himself to the Lord is one spirit with Him. Flee immorality. Every other sin that a man commits is outside the body, but the immoral man sins against his own body. Or do you not know that your body is a temple of the Holy Spirit who is in you, whom you have from God, and that you are not your own? For you have been bought with a price; therefore glorify God in your body" (1 Corinthians 6:17-20). Now, Son, that is pretty straightforward and hard to get around no matter how you interpret Scripture. With this clear command from Christ, let's get a plan on how to accomplish it.

If your bod's God's, He will care how you treat His property! Your body is a treasure! He said: "Food is for the stomach and the stomach is for food, but God will do away with both of them. Yet the body is not for immorality, but for the Lord, and the Lord is for the body" (1 Corinthians 6:13).

> If your bod's God's, He will care how you treat His property!

I know a lot of people who do not believe their body is a treasure. As a matter of fact, most people dislike at least one, if not many, things about their bodies. We complain about our height, weight, hair color, eyes, build, or any number of things Hollywood says is not desirable. God did not die and leave Hollywood in charge of beauty. Even Jesus did not adhere to Hollywood's ideal. The Bible says Jesus was nothing special to look at (Isaiah 53:2). But his body was certainly a gift to us all.

> The Bible says Jesus was nothing special to look at (Isaiah 53:2). But his body was certainly a gift to us all.

Your body is not just your earth suit. It is also a tool. Jesus said: "Do you not know that your bodies are members of Christ?" (1 Corinthians 6:15) Once you become a Christ-follower, you are a tool in the hands of God. This is a big deal. For me, I want to be a tool ready for God to use. That means I must take care of the tool. In prayer I imagine God has this big honkin' tool box, and we're all inside. I want to be in the top drawer, ready when He chooses to pull me out and use me. Does that make sense? If I am weak, sickly, or out of shape, it could seriously limit my ability to be used.

I watched you play football for thirteen seasons. You were only hurt and pulled out of play one time out of all those games, mainly because you took care of your body and were strong and ready. Do it today for God! He wants to put you in a game that is far more important than football.

Do it today for God!

Jesus also said in 1 Corinthians 6:19 that your body is a temple. "Or do you not know that your body is a temple of the Holy Spirit who is in you?" When you became a Christ-follower, your body was invaded by the Holy Spirit. He lives in you right now. Are you taking care of the temple? Far too many ignore this aspect of the Christian life. Many focus on the spiritual side and forget the physical. If you could check the phone book in heaven you would see that the address of the Holy Spirit is in you!

Many focus on the spiritual side and forget the physical.

Your body is a trust. "For you have been bought with a price; therefore, glorify God in your body" (1 Corinthians 6:20). Do you think God was serious when He had Paul write this down? I do! If you borrow something, you should take care of it. Your body is borrowed from God—take care of it. That requires a plan, and it should be very practical. As you grow older this will be so important, and if you start now, you will be glad you did.

In order to stay on top of your health issues, I want you to pay attention to three things: Exercise, Diet and an Annual Physical.

How much do you weigh? What percentage of body fat do you have? Do you think I'm kidding? You should know this. You know the square footage of your house; you know how many gallons of gas your car can hold. You even know how much money is in your bank account. You should know how much excess weight you carry, and you should devise a plan to get rid of it, for the sake of your life, your family, and your role in this world. It is your body; His temple. Maintain it with care.

> You should know how much excess weight you carry, and you should devise a plan to get rid of it, for the sake of your life, your family, and your role in this world.

Look at the sheet enclosed and work out a plan. Like most men, you ignore your health; and you do it to your own peril. As you consider attending to all five of the most important areas I am giving you, do not wait until you feel like it—that may be too late. Do it because it is the right thing to do, not because you feel like it. I made myself exercise even though I did not enjoy it. Please do the same for my future grandkids. I'm sure sorry I missed them.

Exercise—Most people I know think they get enough exercise by having a two-story house, or by pushing a grocery cart through Wal-Mart for 30 minutes a week. But it isn't enough.

Consider the earliest humans. They worked in order to eat. From dawn till dusk, they were hunting, fishing, plowing, planting, hauling water and building their homes and furnishing them by hand. How different the life of a man or woman is today! Everything is done for us. All we have to do is walk a few yards in order to acquire what we need, after we travel there in a climate-controlled car. And sometimes we don't even have to make the little trip to town at all. We can order things online and have them delivered!

> So, in order to be healthy today, exercise must be deliberate.

So, in order to be healthy today, exercise must be deliberate. That includes being specific—how often, how long, where? And what weight do you plan to achieve and maintain?

Son, I know you enjoy running. That puts you a step ahead of most folks. But the next two points might be the most difficult for you!

Diet—Half the food people eat today isn't even food! It might better be called "fillers." People fill up on processed white flour, chips, sugars, sugar substitutes, imitation flavors, guar gums, palm oils and a lot of empty bulk designed to appease the taste buds. Eat these, and the taste buds God gave you will be wasted. He gave them to you so that you can pursue REAL food with REAL flavors—fruits, grains, and vegetables of all kinds. "Then God said, 'Behold, I have given you every plant yielding seed that is on the surface of all the earth, and every tree which has fruit yielding seed; it shall be food for you'" (Genesis 1:29). Did you notice that He gave fruits and vegetables in every color? That's to help you keep variety in your diet! The varying colors give a variety of nutrients. If you vary the colors, you'll achieve more balance—purple beets, orange carrots (vitamin K), green spinach (iron), red strawberries (vitamin C), blueberries, black olives . . .

You've struggled with your weight off and on—and you've done well! But let me tell you by experience, it gets harder as you get older. In my younger days, I could opt for a salad for lunch two days in a row and lose five pounds! Today it's much, much more difficult. And when awareness of weight gain brings on a panic, the tendency is for people to want to shake it off, RIGHT NOW, like a leech or a spider.

> Today it's much, much more difficult.

Yuck! This feeling drives people to fad diets, diets that promise to melt pounds quickly and get you back to your old slim-and-trim self in no time at all! And they work. But when you stop the diet and resume your old habits, the pounds come back, leaving you frustrated. So the key to keeping balance in your weight is by maintaining a diet of variety and moderation, and understanding the values of the foods we eat. Just get yourself informed. Find out what's good for you and what's not, and eat accordingly. It's not rocket science. It's just common sense.

Annual Physical—This is another challenge for many people. They choose not to go to a doctor until they have a symptom of some kind. But an annual physical can reveal problems before they start—high cholesterol, high blood sugar, low iron, low thyroid… these things can be addressed by diet, exercise and mild medications in some cases, thus preventing damage to your organ systems. Don't wait until you feel sick. Set the appointment and keep it. I wish that years ago I had done that. If I had, I could have adjusted my eating and exercise habits sooner. And I might still be with you.

You need to keep an eye on yourself, so you can enjoy a long and happy life. You need a family doctor, and you need to maintain clear communication with him or her. You need to know your family's medical history—tendencies toward heart problems, insulin disorders, even cancer. The purpose of knowing this is not to put fear upon you, but to cause you to do the things that will offset the tendencies. When you have a medical problem, the more quickly you deal with it, the better it will be for you and for your family. So, if you have heart problems in the family—which obviously, you do—then you should take care of your heart and your circulatory system with a bit more attention than other folks. I learned to do what my doctor said after the heart attack. (Hopefully, it will lengthen my days, at least so that I can finish this project!). If cancer runs in the family, have frequent checkups to be a step ahead. In your case, your mother's side of the family has had their share of digestive cancers. So go ahead and have that colonoscopy done every couple years. It doesn't hurt, and it can keep you on top of things. We know that the Lord is still in the healing business, but isn't it sort of irresponsible to follow your appetites into a pit of ill health, pain and fear, and then go running to Him in pain, begging Him to undo 30 years of selfish pigging out? An ounce of prevention really is worth a pound of cure. And a bit of self-control today is better than standing in a prayer line tomorrow.

Planning to Prosper

The next header that appeared on the screen was "Fortune." It reminded me that I hadn't had my cookie. My fortune cookie, from P.F. Chang's. I'd overlooked it. I paused the DVD and dug through the bags, now stuffed with empty Styrofoam greased in duck sauce. My hand grasped a little hard something wrapped in cellophane. Ah, there it was. My fortune.

I knew that's not what Dad meant—but it's what I always used to associate with the word. A cookie, a horoscope, a crystal ball. Luck. Chance. I used to always play this little game with my fortune cookies—Allison started it, I guess. We'd say, "Okay, this is our real fortune!" And then we'd open them, believing in their validity for just a moment. It was fun.

I opened my cookie, as Dad's face was frozen on the screen in an unflatteringly comical expression. He would have laughed at that! He also would have laughed at the words in my fortune cookie:

"Someone from your past will enrich your future."

I don't know what I said there all alone in the room, but it must have included a "Whoa!" or a "No way!" or some reflection of awe. Would God actually speak in a fortune cookie? I laughed. The entire day seemed designed to secure my future in every way. And I had never felt so loved by God—and my Dad.

The resume button brought Dad to life again. And I knew that he was going to tell me something about fortune that would not include "chance" or "luck of the draw." It would be about wisdom and discipline.

DAD CONTINUED:

Priority #4—Your Financial Plan. Son, the first thing you need to know regarding your financial planning is, "Don't confuse your vocation with your financial planning." Your vocation, your career choice, is not a guarantee for success. I guess lots of people who want lots of money study to become doctors or lawyers, or investment bankers, whatever. But the vocation alone isn't the key. It may not be the key at all. Many people with little education have gone on to build great fortunes. That's because there is more to success than formal education.

Fortune is another area of my life that God has blessed beyond my wildest dreams. Sure, I have my associate's degree, and I'm glad for it. But my degree really has little to do with my fortune.

You don't remember our "poor days." Those were before you were born or when you were too young to remember. But you can trust me in this—we had some hard days, financially.

Your mom and I got married in college. She dropped out to work full-time, and I went to college and worked full time. But during those days, you kids were born and we chose for your mom to be a stay-at-home mom. Sure, she could have worked, but the cost of childcare would have used up more than all of her wages. I had to work two jobs to take up the slack. Those were hard days, but we stuck with it—and we stuck with each other—and those days came to be filled with miracles and joy! People would give us garden vegetables the very hour the refrigerator went empty. Or someone would give us a box of disposable diapers their kids outgrew. Everything was right on time.

But even being "poor as church mice" as they say, your mom and I developed a financial plan. And this was the key to fortune—this, and a whole lot of patience and trust! Our goal was to give the Lord 10 percent of our income, save 10 percent, invest 10 percent and live on 70 percent. In a culture of spend-it-all-and-live-on-debt, this was—and is—a hard concept. We missed our goals more than once, especially in the area of saving, but we still strived to keep them the next time.

> In a culture of spend-it-all-and-live-on-debt, this was—and is—a hard concept.

Over the years, you have heard me quote many verses in the Bible about money. This is my favorite. I Timothy 6:7-10 reads, "For we have brought nothing into the world, so we cannot take anything out of it either. If we have food and covering, with these we shall be content. But those who want to get rich fall into temptation and a snare and many foolish and harmful desires which plunge men into ruin and destruction. For the love of money is a root of all sorts of evil, and some by longing for it have wandered away from the faith and pierced themselves with many griefs."

You can see by this that God never said money was evil, He said the "love of money" was evil. I could list so many more verses that deal with money. Money is a great tool, and it gives you many options. It can also present a test from the Lord to see how you will handle it or use it. God can bless you with much money. But you must never forget that you will give an account as to how you used it.

> But you must never forget that you will give an account as to how you used it.

In the New Testament, if you read the words in red, it is very visible how many stories Jesus told for us to be ready to give an accounting of our lives. Romans 14:12 says, "So then each one of us will give an account of himself to God." That seems pretty clear. Indulgence is not going to go over well. Why? Because it's basically selfish. Did you know that sin is selfishness, and selfishness is sin? It's true. Every sin we commit can be traced back to a desire to please or protect ourselves.

Let me read you a story Jesus told in Matthew, Chapter 25. Sit back and allow me to share this story with you. It is serious. It will be like a bedtime story when you were a kid:

> "...For it is just like a man about to go on a journey, who called his own slaves and entrusted his possessions to them. To one he gave five talents, to another, two, and to another, one, each according to his own ability; and he went on his journey. Immediately the one who had received the five talents went and traded with them, and gained five more talents.
>
> In the same manner the one who had received the two talents gained two more. But he who received the one talent went away, and dug a hole in the ground and hid his master's money. Now after a long time the master of those slaves came and settled accounts with them. The one who had received the five talents came up and brought five more talents, saying, 'Master, you entrusted five talents to me. See I have gained five more talents.' His master said to him, 'Well done, good and faithful slave. You were faithful with a few things, I will put you in charge of many things; enter into the joy of your master.'
>
> Also the one who had received the two talents came up and said, 'Master, you entrusted two talents to me…I have gained two more talents.' His master said to him, 'Well done, good and faithful slave. You were faithful with a few things, I will put you in charge of many things; enter into the joy of your master.' And the one also who had received the one talent came up and said, 'Master, I knew you to be a hard man, reaping where you did not sow and gathering where you scattered no seed. And I was afraid, and went away and hid your talent in the ground. See, you have what is yours.' But

his master answered and said to him, 'You wicked, lazy slave, you knew that I reap where I did not sow and gather where I scattered no seed. Then you ought to have put my money in the bank, and on my arrival I would have received my money back with interest. Therefore take away the talent from him, and give it to the one who has the ten talents.' For to everyone who has, more shall be given, and he will have abundance; but from the one who does not have, even what he does have shall be taken away. Throw out the worthless slave into the outer darkness; in that place there will be weeping and gnashing of teeth."

The implications of this story are vast, especially if you believe the Bible, and I know you do. Obviously, the Lord was not happy with the person who lacked the courage and insight to invest his master's money. That servant was dull and self-serving. He chose to play it safe and just do the bare minimum—just hold the money for his master. He didn't think like a businessman, a profitable servant. God has entrusted all of us with gifts and blessings of all kinds. They are ours to hold until His return—but to simply hold them is of no profit to anyone. We are accountable to the Lord for how we use the money we've been given, and for every other thing we have.

> Obviously, the Lord was not happy with the person who lacked the courage and insight to invest his master's money.

People say money buys happiness. And you know what? I can agree with that! Because happiness is temporary. But money can't buy joy. Joy is long-term. Money does bring happiness—happy times, fun, temporary pleasure. Money buys happiness because it gives options, or power to choose. But look at all the people who have won the lottery. Has it brought them joy? Are they filled with contentment and inner peace? Hardly. Happiness is fleeting; it comes and goes, like a thermometer goes up and down. But money just can't buy joy. Joy is that inner contentment—satisfaction; peace. It's like the thermostat. It's set from within, not from without.

You knew of our plan to build four houses over several years, sell each at a profit, invest that profit into the next house, finally to be debt-free by the last one. This gave us a plan and guidelines on creating a budget for the family. This was one of our long-range fiscal goals, and in that economy, thank God it worked! We had several more plans, too, and they have all contributed to the prosperity we enjoy today. As you develop your plan, determine your long, medium and short-term goals. Check the envelope for the Financial Planning list.

> As you develop your plan, determine your long, medium and short-term goals.

[See Appendix]

- Budget

- Giving 10 percent +

- Saving

- Investing/Retirement

With a strong financial plan, 95 percent of your financial questions are answered before they are asked. When you want to spend money or do something that costs, the question is: Is it in the budget? That answers it! This area was not one of my strengths for many years. I spent too much without "counting the cost."

> The question is: Is it in the budget?

Son, as you look back at the long story I read to you, one principle stands out to me: God rewards faithfulness. Watch how the master blesses the slaves who used his money wisely. He was excited and rewarded them richly. I believe God loves to bless His kids.

> God rewards faithfulness

My life is living proof that can't be discounted. I was raised poor, and those first

> I believe God loves to bless His kids.

few years of marriage were hard as I struggled to get into the swing of prosperity. We remember times without groceries, or times the power was almost cut off. But we didn't argue about money because we knew from the start that we would be broke going to school and starting this business. Your mom and I determined early that problems would push us together, not divide us. So, together we faced the finances; it really did put steel in our spines. We were faithful to the Lord to tithe, and then I remember raising it to 20 percent. We didn't tell anyone because they would think we were crazy! How can you be that broke and give 20 percent to the Lord? It depends on your math. We trusted God's old math. We gave to Him and He gave to us; we couldn't out-give Him. There were some years we gave over 50 percent of our income to advance the Kingdom of God. We watched God pour in resources that most would never believe.

> Your mom and I determined early that problems would push us together, not divide us.

> We watched God pour in resources that most would never believe.

Look around, Son. You can see that we are no longer poor. God has blessed us in more ways that we can count. It's as if the Father, Son and Holy Spirit created new ways just to bless me! I am a trophy of God's grace; a testimony of His principle of rewarding faithfulness. Stay faithful to the task and it will amaze you how He will move and the doors He will open.

> It's as if the Father, Son and Holy Spirit created new ways just to bless me!

I looked around at Dad's office. He was right. We were not poor. We didn't live extravagantly, but that was only because he had a strong aversion to waste. He loved beautiful things, though, and lavished Mom with anything she ever wanted. Not surprisingly, she, too, was one to resist the temptation to be wasteful or snooty. Still, I knew she had a Dooney & Bourke bag somewhere, and several rare antique dolls that she enjoyed very much.

Mom and Dad enjoyed the blessings of God. But they also blessed others. If ever there was a balance to be had, they certainly found it. And oh, how I longed to find it, too.

Ch.7

What Will I Be When I Grow Up?

DAD CONTINUED:

Priority #5—Your Vocation. It may seem strange to put this dead last when most people place it first. But among the top five priorities of life, this is the spot where it belongs, on the bottom. Far too many people put it at the number one spot and wonder why life stays messed up. But a vocation or career is simply the means by which you provide food and shelter for your family—so obviously, your family is more important. And since one can't hold down a job without being healthy enough to do the work, it's obvious that fitness trumps vocation, too. And faith, being foundational to life itself, has to be given more attention.

> Far too many people put it at the number one spot and wonder why life stays messed up.

Now, your job is important, if for no other reason than this: You will spend one third of your life there. So choose wisely your vocation. I have heard it said, "If you love your work, you'll never have to work a day in your life." It has been true for me. I was extremely blessed to have a vocation that complimented my purpose

> Now, your job is important, if for no other reason than this: You will spend one third of your life there.

in life. To get paid to do what you love and feel called to do is rare in this world, but it is possible. As much as you love business, this job should do you fine!

If you work hard and prioritize well, God will bless your socks off. He did it for me, and you watched it.

Many people your age don't know what they want to do in life. Perhaps it's because there appear to be so many cushy jobs out there today. Air-conditioned offices, four-day workweeks, paid vacations and huge bonuses are out there. But it's a competitive market. Meanwhile, a person has to work in order to eat, so too many get saddled with jobs they don't enjoy. I know so many young people with college degrees, yet they're working at Taco King, waiting for God to reveal His will for their lives. Others, perhaps like you, keep taking college courses, hoping the golden door will open.

> It's a frustrating place to be.

It's a frustrating place to be.

But I can tell you, if a person, "acknowledges God in all their ways, He will direct their paths" (Proverbs 3:6, paraphrased). He doesn't promise "cushy" or even comfortable. The children of Israel, en route to the land promised to them as Abraham's descendants, spent some years in the desert eating manna—a curious little bead of white that appeared on the ground in the morning. It was the key to their survival for the next 40 years! So why didn't God give His children steak and lobster and fine wine and cheese? They were in process, that's why. They were being taught to trust. It was an essential lesson in the evolution of their culture, for out of that little nation would come the King of Kings! But who would believe it was He? Who would believe that God would send the Messiah

> So why didn't God give His children steak and lobster and fine wine and cheese?

in a cow stall? The same breed of folk who believed He would feed a nation with a little veritable fungus for 40 years—the kind of people who had learned to trust the unseen; those who learned that God's ways aren't man's ways. God has a different scale, a different standard of measure. And His timing is crazy at times! "To everything there is a season" (Ecclesiastes 3:1, paraphrased). There was a time for God's people to enter into the Promise, but they had to wait for it—by enduring hardships, learning to trust and be directed. And not giving up through it all. There was a Promise to those who stuck to it!

> There was a Promise to those who stuck to it!

Some folks complain about being unemployed, and I can understand that. I've also heard a lot of people complain that they hate their jobs. They hate their jobs like Israel hated manna. And they blame it on Adam and or Eve, as if all work is a consequence of the fall of mankind in the Garden of Eden. This cannot be true, since God had already given Adam the job of taking care of the Garden before the first sin. If you go to the third chapter of Genesis you will see that one of the consequences of the sin was that work would be hard. That is part of the "curse" on the planet.

When work is hard, it's hard to find anything in it to like. I even hear it from employees here in our company. It is a very small percentage of people who are happy with their vocations. What a bummer, since a person spends such a big part of his time on the job! And work is where many people try to feed their sense of self-worth and security. Our society adds to the pressure of this priority. When folks met other folks, they used to say, "How do you do?" Now they say, "What do you do?"

> It is a very small percentage of people who are happy with their vocations.

They mean, "Where do you work?" In this culture, we equate who we are with what we do. But remember, who you are depends on far more than the name on the top of your paycheck. You determine who you are by the way you handle all five priorities. So when a person has a "bummer" of a job, he should thank God for the manna while trusting God to direct his path to a personal Promised Land! You don't get there just by trusting, though. You have to move your feet! It takes effort, even to receive The Promise!

> In this culture, we equate who we are with what we do.

Let me give you a thought: rocks are lying all over the ground because we consider them valueless. Otherwise, we'd be picking them up like diamonds. But diamonds, gold, and jewels that we consider of great value must be mined; you have to dig for them. It takes effort. The more valuable something is, normally the more it costs and the harder it is to come by. A good life doesn't fall in one's lap. It may seem that your sudden skyrocketing to a six-figure salary means you have been gifted with an easy life. I can assure you, the money itself is not the secret to the satisfaction you long for. I learned that long ago. And my desire is for you to enjoy life like I have. A huge reason I have loved life is my vocational calling in building this company was so beneficial to so many people—blessing others is a tremendous rush! What an amazing ride it has been. It is my prayer for you that yours is even more thrilling!

> A good life doesn't fall in one's lap.

> Blessing others is a tremendous rush!

Now let me list nine questions to help you chart your course:

1. What is your calling in life?

2. How do you see your future?
   (Or, if it were just like you wanted, what would it look like?)

3. What is the best game plan to get there?

4. What skills will you need to gain to live your plan?

5. What degree or degrees will you need?

6. What goals need to be set, short and long range, for you to live the dream?

7. Who would you enjoy working with? The people on your team are crucial to your achieving your dreams and goals. They will also help determine how much you enjoy your work.

8. Will your work help others? A life lived for others is a life lived well. Working to add value to others makes you feel good when the day is over. Sad is the person who has to work to eat, and hates his or her job. In most surveys given to workers, usually over 50 percent dislike their jobs.

> "When you are making a success of something, it's not work. It's a way of life. You enjoy yourself because you are making your contribution to the world."

9. How can you track your progress? Keep up with the plan and measure yourself against it. Brian Tracy said, *"A clear vision, backed by definite plans, gives you a tremendous feeling of confidence and personal power."* Andy Granatelli summed it up when he said, *"When you are making a success of something, it's not work. It's a way of life. You enjoy yourself because you are making your contribution to the world."*

If you look up the word "work" in the biblical concordance, you will find it used 564 times. The concept of work is a thoroughly Scriptural aspect of everyone's life. You must do what you must do today to get to do what you want to do tomorrow.

> You must do what you must do today to get to do what you want to do tomorrow.

Help people find their purpose—all people. Those at our company and those you meet in your daily life. Help them get to know their own strong suits with aptitude tests and personality tests. Add value to all the people God puts around you. Some you will meet once and never see again. Others will join you in the journey for years. In Luke 6:31, Jesus was clear in that we are to,

> "Treat others the same way you want them to treat you."

"Treat others the same way you want them to treat you." He also pointed out that some of the people we help and care for are angels, of whom we are usually unaware.

Help people find their passions—send them to school, seminars and conferences. Go with them or take them with you. You may lose some to other companies; but you will be adding value to people. This company will continue to flourish and your employees will enjoy working here if you help them find the right vocation.

Mike, if you don't enjoy running this company, please find something else to do! I would work at a job that paid less if I enjoyed it more. Your "job" is your mission field. Your job is a place to work hard and be rewarded

> Your "job" is your mission field.

for it. After a few years here, if you don't think it's God's best for you, tell Josh. There is always a Plan B. Enjoy your work and the people you work with, for, or work for you. I love a picture that author Jim Collins painted for us in this train of thought. He said that you can choose who gets on the bus with you. I want to enjoy the ride so I watch who gets on the bus in our business.

Don't fall prey to destination disease. That's thinking you'll be "happy one day." One day—someday, when you graduate, get married, retire. That isn't right! You must enjoy life today, not just tomorrow! And I know circumstances create variables we cannot control. And it is

> Don't fall prey to destination disease.

during those trying times that we must be like Paul the Apostle, who said, "I know both how to be abased, and I know how to abound: every where and in all things I am instructed both to be full and to be hungry, both to abound and to suffer need" (Philippians 4:12, KJV). But he goes on to say, "I can do all (these) things through Christ which strengtheneth me" (vs. 13).

> "I can do all (these) things through Christ which strengtheneth me."

But there are times when you can do something about your circumstances. The Lord gives you choices on this earth. When you have options, do not wait too long to act upon your freedom to choose. In the book of Wisdom we are warned not to brag about tomorrow, "For we do not know what a day may hold" (Proverbs 27:1, paraphrased). The present moment is the only time you have for certain—it can be gone with the next breath. Life is too short to remain in a dead-end job you really hate. Far too many people feel trapped in their current employment. Sometimes it's part of the perseverance process, like your mother and I had to endure while we were working through school. But if you find yourself miserably unhappy to the point that you cannot recognize the core of joy for the fog in your life, step out in faith. Get a plan to go where you will enjoy your work.

> Life is too short to remain in a dead-end job you really hate.

The Five F's—Faith, Family, Fitness, Fortune and Future—seem to me to be the most important areas of life. I didn't give you a detailed plan for each area; but I gave you an outline to start to work with. The plan and how you live it out is up to you.

> The Five F's—Faith, Family, Fitness, Fortune and Future—seem to me to be the most important areas of life.

Take the sheets in the envelope. The sheets are a starting point. Good luck!

By the way, Son, if you do not want to run the company, I do have options and have planned for that possibility. I don't want you to accept this offer on the simple basis of pleasing me—I would not be pleased. I would never want you to spend your life at a job you hated. I would not want you to miss out on your purpose in life. You have to make the choice for yourself; no one can make it for you. Pick wisely your profession, and your days will be filled with joy.

Motivation is Not Magic

DAD CONTINUED:

Son, we've just covered what I believe are the most important issues of life. You may think everyone knows these principles I've shared with you. You're probably right. Most people know what they ought to do. But knowing what to do isn't the same as doing it. Less than five percent of surveyed Americans have set goals for their lives, and even fewer have plans to achieve them! This has always been an enigma for me. Amazingly, many of my friends see their need, but they refuse to do the work it takes to fill the need. They say, "No thanks; this is a temporary problem. Life will get better." Now, on one hand, they're being positive—even in the way the Apostle Paul said that he had learned how to abound and how to be abased, or how to adapt to life's unforeseen circumstances. But there is another hand… and that is called complacency. Some people want to just "wait on God" and let Him do all the work to make things happen in their lives. But you can't just apply positive thinking, grunt, or even wish upon a star and wait for God to perform His magic tricks for you. "Waiting

> Most people know what they ought to do. But knowing what to do isn't the same as doing it.

> "No thanks; this is a temporary problem. Life will get better."

on God" can have a whole 'nuther connotation, to borrow a phrase from your grandmother. To see this in action, go down to Outback Steakhouse. Once you're seated, a guy or girl will come up to your table and set down a couple of glasses of water. This is part of "waiting on you." They ask what they can do for you, what you would like to order, whether you would like dessert. What would your dinner be like if they just plopped down next to you with their pad and pencil and just waited for your Delmonico steak and bloomin' onion to appear magically? You see, waiting on God requires action. There may be times when waiting is just that—waiting; like, when your date can't make up her mind between the Caesar salad and the house salad, and everyone just sits there while the Final Jeopardy theme song plays in your head. Sometimes we must wait for God to move—but that is when our hands are completely tied, and we require a supernatural stirring of events. But aside from those times of "standing still and seeing the salvation of the Lord," as in Exodus 14:13, we must act; and action requires motivation.

> Waiting on God requires action.

So how can one become motivated? Wow, Son, if I could put motivation in a pill or even in a program, I would be the richest guy on the planet! Motivation comes hard. That's because motivation has to come from within. And if you don't have it, you can't get it without some other stimuli.

> Motivation comes hard. That's because motivation has to come from within.

Some folks depend on drugs or alcohol to "lift the spirits" enough to get motivated. But that results in entrapment and bondage. It's a false motivation.

"Lifting the spirits" is another word for hope, I guess. When people feel happy, they feel hopeful. But "happy" comes and goes with life's ups and downs. As I said before, it's like a thermometer. Happiness reacts to externals. Joy, on the other hand, is internal, and is steady, even when times are tough. It is a kind of hope. It is a long-lasting "lifting of the spirit." And it does not come from drugs, or alcohol, or even from the love of a woman, or the pleasure of children. Joy comes from knowing who you are, and knowing Whose you are, and knowing that those facts cannot change. When you find that joy, you will begin to find your motivation.

Finding that joy is not easy. Knowing who you are and to Whom you belong is a lifelong study. We get better at it as we go along. But the "knowing who you are" aspect is recognizing your own power to DO. It is a Divine gift to you. You have power to choose; you have power to act. You have power to team up with God. Let Him lead, and be His active co-laborer!

We truly reap what we sow. And if we sow nothing, we reap nothing. So many here at the company could have had a better life, but they refused to do the work. I'm talking about planning and sticking to a plan to get their families out of debt, into good health, into harmony and communication with one another. You can't plant wheat if you want to harvest corn. You really do reap what you sow. It is impossible to ignore that biblical principal without disappointment.

> If we sow nothing, we reap nothing.

> It is impossible to ignore that biblical principal without disappointment.

When you shoot at nothing, you'll hit it every time! So please, Son, don't aim at nothing. Take careful aim at life and develop goals and a plan to achieve! Most people who leave life to chance aren't very happy about how it ends, and then they wonder why it all turned out so badly. Then begins the blame game, and they enter the moan zone!

I know what I'm laying out for you is not easy. Yet, all that is required is small amounts of daily discipline. There will be times when you feel like it's all going nowhere. There are times when you'll want to quit, to just give up. But if you give in to discouragement, you'll begin to vegetate in front of the TV or computer screen, or waste away playing a video game. It's easy to be distracted from important disciplines when you're weary. I have watched many throw their goals and plans out the window because they didn't ride that bucking bull through the hard times. Instead, they let weariness and lethargy swallow them up. They gave their precious time to idleness, in the name of "rest" or "relaxation." Giving up isn't rest. It's transferring energy to something less profitable.

> It's easy to be distracted from important disciplines when you're weary.

Everybody faces discouragement. Weariness comes when you feel like you're pedaling through life, just spinning your wheels on slick pavement, going nowhere. What do you do when your motivation goes AWOL? How do you escape the quagmire that catches and keeps most people? Your number one recourse is prayer. This should already be a daily routine laid out in your growth plan. Never let it leave your heart and mind that God is the source of all power and positive motivation. He will supernaturally give you enough to keep you going, like the manna in the desert. It may still feel grievous for a while, but it will be enough. His grace is sufficient. And you will grow so strong in character through these times!

> Your number one recourse is prayer.

I pray many biblical prayers. One stands out at this juncture, a prayer that has helped me many times. It's Psalm 51:12, "…sustain me with a willing spirit." A loose translation is, "God, make me want to!" King David prayed this prayer. Psalm 51 is actually a prayer of confession—his confession. David had committed adultery and murder. Those are serious sins in anyone's book. And God's prophet had just confronted Him about it. So in the prayer David tells God how

> "God, make me want to!"

sorry he is; how far away from God he is. Realizing and admitting his propensity to sin, he longs to be in a right relationship with God. He knows it will require a desire for righteousness above all else.

He doesn't want to blow it again, but he also knows that the heart of a man is desperately wicked at its core and he can't be good on his own. So, he prays, "Make me want to!" He looks to the Lord even to give him a right heart! It reminds me of the man in Mark 9:24, who had a measure of faith that Jesus could heal his sick child, but he knew his faith wasn't perfect. He said, with tears, "...I do believe; help my unbelief!" God will meet you where you are; he'll take up the slack. But it is your responsibility to humble yourself and ask.

> He knows it will require a desire for righteousness above all else.

It is also essential that you recognize the gravitational pull of this culture and of sin itself. The pull or current I'm talking about is the negative and pessimistic outlook and attitude that surrounds us. It will carry you downstream without any effort on your part. As a matter of fact, it requires quite a bit of effort just to stay in place with the current going the wrong way. To make any advance against it requires rowing with all your might. Without setting a strong guard on your heart and mind, you will give up and let the culture of sin swallow you. Some of the ideas that pull at you are things that make you feel like this whole God and faith thing is just too much trouble for the amount of good that comes out of it. You've heard these things all your life from people who'd rather take the easy road to destruction than the hard road to success:

> It requires quite a bit of effort just to stay in place with the current going the wrong way.

"There's no use, it won't work!"

"It's been tried before!"

"It will cost too much."

"It will take too much time!"

"You'll make people mad!"

"Don't stir up the water!"

And there are a thousand more excuses and reasons why you should not even attempt to grow and be better in life. Every change I made was met with conflict, and the same will be true for you. Growth is not easy. You need to turn on the "spin cycle of success" in growth in your life: CHANGE, CONFLICT, and then CHAOS. And then the cycle starts over! Expect it! Be ready!

> You need to turn on the "spin cycle of success" in growth in your life.

Do you remember how they train elephants at the circus? When they are young they are chained up to stout tree stumps. Try as the baby might, it can't break the chain free. Later when the animal is full-grown and fully capable of breaking the chain, it refuses to try. It has been conditioned—trained that it can't. So, they can tie the huge beast to a twig and he stands in place, never moving forward. The elephant believes it is hopeless. How sad for the elephant and millions of people in the same plight. It doesn't have to be so for you.

> The elephant believes it is hopeless.

As a matter of fact, Son, you are a blessed man. That is how you are to face the world and your future. With an attitude of gratitude and the knowledge you can or you'll die trying. I told your mom to put on my tombstone, "At least he tried." See to that, Son!

This lesson is so important and is missed by millions. No matter which way you go in life, it will be tough and hard to stay motivated. In the midst of the messiness and difficulty of life most will be looking for the easy way out! It doesn't exist. We can go all the way back to the Garden of Eden when God promised Adam in Genesis 3:19, "By the sweat of your face you will eat bread." Let me paraphrase that for you: Life and work will be hard. The quicker you comprehend this,

> In the midst of the messiness and difficulty of life most will be looking for the easy way out! It doesn't exist.

the better off in life you will be. You will at least be prepared to face the trials life can and does dish out.

It might not be easy, but trust me—it can be done! You've got to turn to God from the beginning, not when you hit critical mass. Ask the Creator of positive thinking and faith to give you a vision, an inner revelation of cause-and-effect, the kind that will make you want to take action and execute every step of that plan! Basically, Son, we humans usually do what we want to. So, as God grants your prayer, which is His will expressed in His Word, you will discover that you actually want to keep going forward with Him.

This is the time to draw strength from the Lord in maintaining your daily disciplines and personal growth plan. Too many people forget about a relationship with God until problems pop up. Without developing a quality devotional life you won't know His

> Without developing a quality devotional life you won't know His voice when you need to hear it.

voice when you need to hear it. You also won't know His Word well enough for you to get insight or answers when you desperately need them. Daily disciplines are sort of like the two-a-days before football season. I know you remember them. Practice is preparation for the "Friday Night Lights" of life.

Please hear my heart, Son; this is important. When I feel my "want to" waning, I go to God. Sometimes I pull away from other things for extra time with the Lord. Since we are Christ-followers, we follow His example. While Jesus was on earth, He frequently stole away for personal prayer retreats. Prayer was the only spiritual discipline the disciples asked Jesus to teach them. They asked because it was obvious prayer was the secret to His strength. Remember how Samson's strength was in his hair? You have a source of strength, too, Son (and I can assure you, it's not in your hair!). His name is Jesus! Let Him be your rock and anchor. Your faith and growth in God must be your number one priority.

> Prayer was the only spiritual discipline the disciples asked Jesus to teach them.

In addition to prayer, you need to fortify yourself by remembering your past victories. Many times as I sought the Lord for "want to" motivation, I've taken a look back at all the miracles, all the "God stuff" that has happened in my life. So when the world affixed its claws into my mind, trying to pull me back to how I used to live, I remembered the multitude of miracles that God had done for us. That is what God always tried to do for Israel throughout the Old Testament. Remember Exodus, the Red Sea, Moses, manna, miracles? The Lord told those people to save some of the manna, and other mementos, to be put in the Ark of the Testimony. Why? So they could look at them during the hard times and remember that God always comes through! As they looked at those things, they would remember who they were, and Whose they were! They were God's chosen! Who could stand against them? That Ark was their motivation—their cheerleader! You have your own collection of events that testify to God's hand in your life. Look back into your

> So when the world affixed its claws into my mind, trying to pull me back to how I used to live, I remembered the multitude of miracles that God had done for us.

own "Ark of the Testimony" now and then; it will testify to you of God's faithfulness. He will never forsake you.

Let me peek back into mine for a moment. When your mom and I were young, so many stormy winds of adversity blew into our lives— God saw our family through each and every one. We grew stronger in our faith daily. I remember when you were four years old. We had just moved to Louisiana. I wasn't making

> Look back into your own "Ark of the Testimony" now and then; it will testify to you of God's faithfulness. He will never forsake you.

much money, and your mom was home with three small kids. To make matters worse, we had no health insurance. Then you got sick. We didn't know what was wrong, but literally, your gums turned black and bled continually. You couldn't eat or brush your teeth. I didn't know what to do—I could barely put food on the table, let alone dole out any money for a doctor. I felt like such a failure as a father. All I could do was hold you in my arms and cry out to God. We both cried. And I asked God for another miracle. Son, He came through! You probably don't remember the incident, but I do. God answered. I had become friends with a doctor, and when he heard what was happening, he gave me some sample antibiotics for you.

> If you ask this same God, He will sustain you through every storm! He loved you then; He loves you now.

That medicine went to work quickly, and soon all symptoms had disappeared! I couldn't have afforded the medicine or the visit to the doctors' office, but God provided a means whereby you could be healed. If you ask this same God, He will sustain you through every storm! He loved you then; He loves you now.

I don't want you to get the idea that you can do any of this motivation stuff on your own. While you're the only one who can make your life choices, you must remember that you need a support system in order to stay motivated—this support system is made up of people who can strengthen you, encourage you, cheer you on, reminding you that you can make it; reminding you that God is with you!

You need your family, of course. But you also need friends. You need a church. You need counselors—people who know God, too, and know of His ability to work things out for us and with us.

I have watched so many people in trouble go to the wrong counselors—people who don't really see the whole spiritual picture. Maybe some people think they have nowhere else to turn so they let their fingers do the walking instead of their heart and they start flipping through the Yellow Pages. But let me tell you, if you want the mind of the Lord, you go to someone who knows Him. If you are having marriage problems, you don't want to go to someone with a wrecked marriage or a string of divorces behind them. You go to someone with a long-lasting, great marriage! If you have money problems, you won't seek counsel from a company facing bankruptcy. If you want to learn to hunt, find someone who has antlers hanging over their fireplace. Pick a fishing buddy who has a lunker hanging on the wall! My point is really this: be careful who speaks into your life. Seek counsel from someone who believes in the saving power of Jesus Christ; one who values the counsel of the Holy Spirit.

> I have watched so many people in trouble go to the wrong counselors

> Be careful who speaks into your life.

So when your "want to" wanes (and it will), pray! Go to your "Ark of the Testimony" and recall past victories and miracles. Seek support and the confidence of another believer.

One last thing I always do is to meditate on the Lord's life here on earth. No luxuries, no home to call His own, few friends and a fickle crowd. One day those people sang His praise and the next they screamed, "Crucify Him!" I think about His love and the pain He endured. Being crucified was a horrible death. Think of His suffering for us—you and me. Do you remember watching the movie, *The Passion of the Christ*? Watch it again. It will remind you that Jesus never gave up on us. Let's not give up on Him.

> Don't allow yourself to be pulled under by the riptide of society.

Stand strong, Son! Don't allow yourself to be pulled under by the riptide of society. You have a plan. Work it! Remember when we watched your favorite team, the Colts, play in the Super Bowl? At halftime the Colts were down at a deficit that was historically insurmountable. Yet when the game was over, the Colts were victorious! During the interviews Coach Dungee was asked about his halftime talk. He had told the team to "stay the course." They had a game plan and they stuck with it. So should you. Stick with it! Don't let the devil dissuade, deter or delay you.

> "Stay the course."

Remember there will always be many negative voices—please be careful. Choose your inner circle wisely. Choose people that will "speak the truth in love." And pick people that will stoke your fire, not soak it!

> Remember there will always be many negative voices.

So, when your "wanter" doesn't want to, remember:

- Pray
- Remember Past Victories
- Go to Trusted Friends for Encouragement
- Find a Good, Positive Thinking Book or CD
- Remember the Life of the Lord

- Take a Prayer Pause—Retreat!

Remember what Nehemiah said, *"The joy of the Lord is our strength"* (Nehemiah 8:10). And remember that "I don't want to" never did anything!

Feelings are as Fickle as the Wind

DAD CONTINUED:

Something you have said to me often, Son, "But Dad, I don't feel like it." Few people do feel like it! As you look around at people, do they look tired to you? You live in a day when technology is multiplying daily. Labor saving devices are developed and deployed at a rapid pace. Yet people are tired. This feeling pulverizes people's growth. I say it because most people are led by their feelings. This is a huge tactical error.

> Yet people are tired. This feeling pulverizes people's growth.

Since feelings are in charge, few people engage in prioritizing growth activities that will aid them in the future. Most people feel overworked, feel overwhelmed, and feel so tired they can only think about today. "Look at my to-do list. There is no way to get it all done. I'm tired just thinking about it." This is the cry of our culture. "If I can just get home and lounge in our La-Z-Boy I'll be alright."

> "If I can just get home and lounge in our La-Z-Boy I'll be alright."

You and I both know this is true because we have both felt the same way. Often I have told you not to allow your feelings to be the engine of your life. If you were a train, your emotions should be the caboose. Most people allow their lives to be controlled by their feelings. Now, feelings are a fantastic gift from God that enhance many life experiences. Enjoy them. But God never intends for you to depend on them, any more than you can trust the wind He created. Feelings are as fickle as the wind. And if you follow them like most people, you can easily spend your life chasing your tail.

You must put His will as the engine that pulls the train—the one in charge. Hopefully, Son, you will always surrender your will to the Lord. So your daily decisions, directions, and discernment are from your will, not how you feel at the moment. Your feelings can be cool as long as they are the caboose of the train. They follow. They line up with your will. Remember if your feelings get in control, they can't be trusted. How many feel like crafting a personal growth plan? And fewer than that actually feel like following through. Who feels like daily disciplines? Who wants to get up early to exercise? (Sick people!) Who feels like getting up early to pray or read their Bible? Who wants to pass up Baskin-Robbins or Krispy Kreme without stopping? Feelings always want to be fed with whatever they feel like.

> You must put His will as the engine that pulls the train—the one in charge.

> Feelings always want to be fed with whatever they feel like.

After coming home from a tiring and stressful day at work, who feels like reading a book? That requires focus and energy you don't feel you have. What we feel like is vegetating in front of the TV watching our favorite show. Studies show the average American spends four hours a day in front of the TV. Not a quality investment of time, but Hollywood

> Studies show the average American spends four hours a day in front of the TV. Not a quality investment of time, but Hollywood appreciates it.

appreciates it. We all know how concerned Hollywood is with your future! What if you take just one of your TV hours per day and apply it to your personal growth? Reading books that will help you grow—nonfiction. What about studying or starting another degree online? Pursue the things, Son, which will grow you and prepare you to be better. Feed your mind and spirit, not just your feelings.

When opportunity knocks, it is too late to prepare for it. What's one hour out of every 24? Think about this: In one year you would invest 365 hours toward growth. That is 15 ½ days a year. You may think that's not too much. But how many actually do it? Just think of that one hour a day over the course of a year—with compounding interest. It will blow your mind, Son, at what God could and would do with that investment. Isaiah 40:30-31 says, "Though youths grow weary and tired, and vigorous men stumble badly, yet those who wait for the Lord will gain new strength; they will mount up with wings like eagles, they will run and not get tired, they will walk and not become weary." A whole new world opens up for that kind of person.

Then why doesn't everyone do it, you ask? I have wondered that many times myself. The bottom line is that they don't feel like it. Without question, the legions are led by their feelings.

> Without question, the legions are led by their feelings.

When I was sixteen years old I bought a 1966 convertible Corvette. Oh yeah. That car was my pride and joy. My grandmother helped me buy it. It was a head-turner, and the girls lined up to take rides. I had that car about two years when the radiator developed a leak. You know what—I didn't feel like fixing it. I rationalized and justified that I didn't have the money or the time. So I let it go.

Every few days I had to add water to the radiator. The leak wasn't that bad. Now in retrospect, removing it and repairing it would have been easier, and inexpensive. But remember, I didn't feel like it. So I continued the bizarre behavior of looking for water to fill the radiator. Many times I was caught out with no station available. At those times the car would inevitably overheat. This is not good for an engine. You would think I would have seen the pitiful pattern and taken care of business. Wrong. Nope, not me. I didn't want to. I didn't feel like it.

You can probably guess the outcome—yes, a blown engine! With just a few hours I could have repaired the radiator. The cost would have been minimal. Now it would take weeks and cost thousands! If I didn't have the $25 for the repair, where was I going to acquire thousands? Pay now or pay later. Later, costs more. Yeah, I should

> Pay now or pay later.
> Later, costs more.

have learned my lesson about putting feelings in front, but sadly, it would require more sore lessons. That's what today is for, Son. Learn off my dime. Please!

When you and your brother were very young I always had a project around the house. As I recall, you guys were never excited about them. It meant work to do when you wanted to play with your friends or, as you grew older, cruise the roads. Most of your friends rarely had to work at home and clearly didn't comprehend why you did. Today I hope you see the wisdom in our work. There was a method to the madness. I was trying to prepare you to know how to work.

> Plan the work and
> work the plan.

There was always a bigger plan afoot. Your mom and I planned to build four houses and end up debt-free. Work, yes, but well worth it in the end. I hope you get it now. Plan the work and work the plan.

Remember when your friends would spend the night? You always had to have a gang—a posse. I usually made them work or go home! Many of them thought I was too strict and that you and your brother were slaves. You usually agreed with them. But it wouldn't take me five minutes to tell which of your friends had to work at home. Most had no idea of how to work and usually looked for any excuse to exit the project. Although you had no idea, it really was comical to watch!

One of the guys obviously had no idea how to work and told me his dad said his only job was to make good grades. (Good thing that wasn't your job.) He said his dad wouldn't allow him to help around the house. Good thing he hung around—he learned a lot working at our house. But wow, did all of you gripe!

Now look at you. You've applied yourself to knowledge. And, better yet, you know how to work. You're certainly not lazy. All your life I tried to teach you to work hard regardless of how you felt. You really did get it, and I'm so proud. It was to prepare you for today. The teaching, pushing, fussing and encouragement were for now. I loved you too much to let you be lazy. You are too gifted and talented not to maximize all you can be. Your future is too great for you to be a couch potato! Turn off the TV and pick up a book. Pursue with passion your Personal Growth Plan.

> Your future is too great for you to be a couch potato! Turn off the TV and pick up a book. Pursue with passion your Personal Growth Plan.

Just a couple more thoughts on flying by your feelings. When you were a teenager, I decided to learn to fly. So I signed up and took flying lessons. Besides becoming a safe and proficient pilot, I learned some other valuable lessons. My favorite was flying by faith, not feelings.

Early into the lessons the instructor taught me how to fly without looking outside the cockpit. "Everything you need, Sir, is right in front of you. These gauges will supply you with all the information necessary to navigate. But feelings, Sir, will get you killed." I was all ears.

There is a problem that can occur in the clouds. It is called spatial disorientation. In common terms it means you can't tell up from down. Believe me, it is true. So regardless of how you feel, fly by the gauges.

> "But feelings, Sir, will get you killed."

Many pilots have been killed in crashes due to following their feelings. They are in the clouds and the gauges all read that the plane is descending at a rapid rate. But the pilot feels certain he is ascending. Now the crucial decision—feelings or gauges—you must choose. If the pilot decides to reject the information from the plane and fly by his or her feelings, the flight will end in a fiery crash on the ground. Remem-

> Now the crucial decision—feelings or gauges—you must choose.

ber, you can look out the window, but no visual references are available to aid you. Son, never fly by feelings.

For me, since I was twenty-two years old, the Bible has been my guiding gauge. I have learned to fly by faith, not feelings. Remember, I said before, your feelings are as fickle as the wind. Trust the gauges. Stay on track with your G.P.S. (God's Positioning System), or your feelings can lead you to a fiery crash in your life!

This is what happened to King Solomon. Now there was a guy packed with potential who ended in failure. This guy had it all—power, potential and position. He was made King of Israel near the death of his dad, King David. When he was crowned king, he became the most powerful man alive! Israel was the military might of the Eastern world. No one dared challenge Solomon. David left him wealth, power and 21 billion in today's money to build the Tabernacle. For him life was good and soon to get better. The dude had 700 wives and 300 shack-ups. And the equivalent of one THOUSAND mothers-in-law!

Soon after he took the reign, God showed up in a dream. God asked Solomon what he needed. A blank check from Heaven! Choose wisely...he did. He asked the Lord to give him wisdom to lead the nation. God was impressed with him. He granted him not only to be the wisest man ever, but also gave him riches and fame even though he didn't ask for them.

Now that is what I call a super start for a career! Yet with all he had, upon his death he had drifted away from God and had become an idol worshipper. He chose to fly by feelings, not faith and the gauges God had given. Not only did he finish badly, but he also helped Israel to start on a downward spiral spiritually. The country began a bitter civil war and lost the favor it had enjoyed.

Again, feelings are O.K., Son, as long as they're the caboose and not driving the train. Just remember, they can kill you. "I don't feel like it" is a real killer. But you know to keep pushing through the feeling, Son, and you know it's not easy. I have watched you push through in many

> "I don't feel like it" is a real killer.

situations. I saw the opposing football team "triple-team" you to keep you out of the backfield. But you got in. Always push through, regardless of how you feel.

Ch.10

The Microwave Mentality

I couldn't believe it was 9:30. Between watching and pausing, rewinding, replaying, crying and eating, I had spent seven hours there with Dad. Wow! All of this was a little too surreal. I had to take a breather. My head was spinning with memories, and now all of this new perspective…Dad was right. I probably wouldn't have listened if he'd told me all this before. In fact, he HAD told me all these things before, in the course of life. I'd ignored most of it. It was Dadspeak—the kind of stuff that goes into a kid's ear and out the other. But now, with Dad gone, I longed for his counsel. I hung onto his every word. I wondered whether that's how the disciples felt when the Master was taken from them. Jesus' words became treasures to be written and recorded and passed down to all generations.

> It was Dadspeak—the kind of stuff that goes into a kid's ear and out the other.

I got back in Dad's big chair and reached for the mouse and clicked the screen back to life. There he was again. What a gift he was to me!

DAD CONTINUED:

Son, I remember back in 1986, your mom and I got our first microwave oven! What a fancy schmancy gizmo that was! Instead of having to boil a kettle of water, your mom could brew her cup of tea in one minute! A cold biscuit became steamy hot in 15 seconds! What an invention!

Today, the microwave epitomizes the quick fix. Everything is fast. Fast food drive-thrus, high-speed internet connections…we complain about how "slow" our computers are, when just a few years ago we'd been happy to wait ten whole minutes for some of the information we now snap up in a matter of seconds.

The "microwave mentality" has spoiled us. And it has spread to the way we do business. We want everything quickly. Like, right now! We want it all right now—health, wealth, wisdom, family, and a great walk with God. We also want every-thing, all the stuff that goes with it. But some things still require time, and always will.

> The "microwave mentality" has spoiled us.

This is why plans and processes are so vital. Plans work with time—little imperceptible improvements over time that compound into amazing accomplishments. These improvements will, or at least can happen in all five of the areas of importance in your life.

Let's think of it with a monetary mindset, just to make a point. A young man like you starts to invest a small percentage into an investment account. If you watch the account daily, not much will happen, but if you put that little bit of money in on a monthly basis, over your lifetime the increase will be incredible. You will

> This is why plans and processes are so vital. Plans work with time—little imperceptible improvements over time that compound into amazing accomplishments.

have more than enough to retire on! If a twenty-year-old invests $20 a week at 10 percent interest, in 45 years he'd have almost a million dollars to live on. In financing there is the law of 72 months. Your money should double every 72 months with a good interest rate. It seems like magic—but it requires time in order to work.

This same magic can work against you. For instance, when you buy a car. It might seem great to make small monthly payments on a car over a long period of time, but you can end up essentially paying for a car and a motorcycle by the time you add up the interest!

When some people today shop for a car they don't ask how much the car costs. No, today it is, "How much are the payments?" People can make small payments that easily fit into their monthly (short-term, "microwave mentality"!) budgets. The lending industry loves this! It makes their world go 'round. Because if you buy with credit you will ALWAYS pay far more than the sticker price. Why? It's that simple yet profoundly powerful concept called interest—or better yet, compounding interest.

> No, today it is, "How much are the payments?"

Always remember that money's not everything, but you use it to buy almost everything, so money is important. If you will notice, in every town or city you visit, the biggest and most ornate buildings are banks. This is the case because they have most of the money. They have most of the money because they have learned to use the power of interest. Together let's learn a valuable lesson from the bank. You can earn interest or pay interest! Remember, life is all about choices!

> Remember, life is all about choices!

See, in your life you can let interest work for you or against you. This lesson is about so much more than finance; it covers every area that matters most in your life. Life is about compounding interest. As I have said before, you can pay now and play later, or you can play now and pay later. If you pay later, you will pay more because you will be charged interest.

When your mom and I built our first house we had to borrow the money for the lot and cost of construction. I almost went into shock when the banker showed me how much I would pay over the life of the loan. It is a law they have to disclose to you. It was two or three times what I was borrowing. The magic of compound interest… That was working in the bank's favor, not mine; it's a great reason to try to live debt-free. That was when your mom and I came up with the plan to get out of debt.

We can apply the principle of interest to all the areas of priority in our lives. Over the years the cumulative effect and growth will be amazing. The Apostle Paul said, "…*on the other hand, discipline yourself for the purpose of godliness…*" (1 Timothy 4:7). By its very nature, discipline requires time.

> Over the years the cumulative effect and growth will be amazing.

"Take pains with these things; be absorbed in them, so your progress will be evident to all" (1 Timothy 4:15). Even the word "progress" implies that an element of time is involved.

So disciples are not made in a day, but daily. Daily, discipline must be applied to important areas of growth. It's like making deposits into a bank. It grows and accrues interest.

> It's like making deposits into a bank. It grows and accrues interest.

It's important to start the process early in life, not later. By the time most people understand the need for daily discipline, it is too late to get the ballooning effect of interest. But starting later in life is better than never starting at all. Most people, Son, are focused only on the present—what the microwave of life can cook up for them now. They miss out on God's best for them.

The principles of patience and discipline helped me build this business one sale, and one client at a time,

> They miss out on God's best for them.

working hard and building a little each day. That, Son, is how you grow a life. Slowly. Slowly you will gain understanding, ability, speed, insight and maturity. It won't happen by accident or magic. No, it won't happen easily!

Sounds like serious work, Son, all these processes and plans. But there's no way around them. As you make growth plans, make sure you know you're in it for the long haul. That's vision. Don't be one of those persons who sets their short-term goals too high and long-term goals too low, or you'll set yourself up for disappointment.

> Don't be one of those persons who sets their short-term goals too high and long-term goals too low, or you'll set yourself up for disappointment.

A good example of this can be seen in folks who attempt the great feat of personal weight loss. It takes a long time even to get motivated for such an undertaking, but the anticipation of a summer cruise or a class reunion usually fuels the challenge. So they pick a plan and set a goal—say, one pound a day for a month. "Yes, I believe I can lose 30 lbs. this month. I'll be ready for summer." So what happens in 30 days? You guessed it—they miss the goal. Discouragement sets in, and even depression.

The problem is that the goal was too high. The only way to lose one pound a day is to just not eat at all! The short-term goal was unrealistic. Now what about four ounces daily? That doesn't sound like much, but it's about 1.5 lbs. a week—much more attainable. And to drop 30 lbs., a person needs five months, not one!

> The problem is that the goal was too high.

Personal growth is the same way. You develop a plan and work it daily. You won't become the Apostle Paul in a week but you will grow and enjoy the journey! I know it's hard, but it works.

Let me remind you of my life story again—it will help you see how the interest grows over the years.

My mom and dad split when I was three years old, when your Uncle Rick was just born. Life was tough for us kids. I was sexually and physically abused as a little boy. I spent some of my early years in the housing projects on the bad side of town. I smoked my first joint at age 10. Yes, marijuana. Now, who would give drugs to a ten-year-old kid? My step-uncle! By the time I was 18, pot

> I was an addict. It was easy to get there, just rolling with the flow of life. But it was hard to get out.

was nothing. I had gone on to harder things. I was an addict. It was easy to get there, just rolling with the flow of life. But it was hard to get out. Just remember, sin will take you farther than you planned to go, keep you longer than you planned to stay, and cost you more than you were planning to pay.

My heart was empty. I was discouraged and depressed. I make no excuses, Son. Getting high made me feel good, so I did it any way I could. I became a serious addict and a drug dealer. Needle marks ran in a dotted pattern up and down both arms. It was miraculous how the Lord protected me from death or disease. I used more dirty needles than I want to think about.

My worst fear during that time was being alone. I began to hate my life, my sin, the emptiness. Still today, decades after my deliverance and full forgiveness, the sins I committed haunt my mind.

At the age of 22, I experienced an overdose. I ended up in Memorial Hospital. I had wrecked my young life. What could I do? Where could I turn for help? There, Son, I made the best decision I had ever made. I did what millions had done before me—I

> I did what millions had done before me—I cried out to God, my last and only hope.

cried out to God, my last and only hope. Remember, I had not grown up in church like you, Son. I knew virtually nothing about God or the Bible. All I knew how to do was ask Jesus to save me—to pick up the broken pieces of my life. Wow! I had no idea of what to expect. But right there He transformed me. It was more than awesome! Words

> And what a gift! I felt like a new person with a new heart. Free as a bird!

can't describe it. Right there He removed every desire I had for drugs. It was His grace, I know that. Just a gift. And what a gift! I felt like a new person with a new heart. Free as a bird! The burdens of a lifetime were gone in an instant. Son, I felt clean; deep-down clean. My meeting God in the hospital wasn't a quick fix—it was the spiritual eye-opener and new start I needed to follow His plan to a transformed life!

I had no idea of what I was in for. Remember, Son, I wasn't much. I was just a broken young man climbing out of a hospital bed. One thing I found out early is that God doesn't need much. He delivered me instantly and completely, without a grunt or a strain. And why not? This

> He parted the Red Sea with a stick and fed 5,000 with a Happy Meal.

is God I'm talking about! He parted the Red Sea with a stick and fed 5,000 with a Happy Meal. And this same God healed my life and gave me a jump-start for a full life of joy. Jesus said, "I came to give you life, life more abundant" (John 10:10, paraphrased). His eternal words are still echoing today. And He means it.

I left that hospital a rich man in spirit. But what did I have in the natural? Nothing. Years of drug abuse and back alley deals rendered nothing. No deposits, no returns. I had "sown" nothing good, so it would be a while before I "reaped." But God is so good and full of grace that things quickly got better. He supplied everything I needed. I found a church full of folks who loved me—the support system I told you about. And I didn't abuse that support. I did my part to become self-sufficient, and I soon became one of the givers, myself! And that, Son, is life!

Oh…I may have forgotten to tell you that I flunked out of college the first time, before I turned my life over to Jesus and learned the value of personal discipline. By applying His principles—and with His supernatural gift of grace!—I went on to college, had a family, and

> This washed-up druggie got a life!

earned a degree. What a blessing! This washed-up druggie got a life! I promise you, no one would have "thunk it." But I can't stress to you enough the fact that the process took years, and I never stopped growing.

Now, three decades, later I am still growing. Slowly, imperceptibly, and daily I grow. It requires a plan of daily disciplines. The interest really adds up after many years. You know, Son, I'm glad you never knew me in my "old days," my time as a junkie. I'm still thanking God for His rescue in the hospital. I'm a satisfied customer. Just think, if I came this far from that low, where can you go from where you are? Launch off into your potential from my shoulders, Son! It is what I've tried to prepare you for since you were born. Since you did not experience the dark side like I did, I believe you can soar higher than I ever hoped I could.

You know, Son, I'm sure I'm having a great day in Heaven today. I wish I could tell you all I see and smell! "…Things which eye has not seen and ear has not heard and which has not entered into the heart of man, all that God has prepared for those who love Him" (1 Corinthians 2:9). Love the Lord, Mike. It's easy if you know Him. And you can know Him by hanging out with Him. Talk to Him. Pray. Apply yourself to be the best you can be! And be patient to see the results!

_____

"We do not want you to become lazy, but to imitate those who through faith and patience inherit what has been promised" (Hebrews 6:12, NIV).

It's Your Call

"You, therefore, who teach another, do you not teach yourself?"
–Romans 2:21(a)

DAD CONTINUED:

This segment holds a lesson that is mega-important for you. It is not just important that you hear it, but it must become a part of you, your ethos; your heart; your psyche; your person. It's about responsibility—owning up to your weaknesses, moving forward in spite of them.

> This mentality will guarantee the failure of a person, a family, a culture and a nation.

You surely know that you live in a culture of entitlements. "It's not my fault. Someone owes me. Someone needs to pay for me. Someone take care of me." This mentality will guarantee the failure of a person, a family, a culture and a nation. It reflects a lack of personal responsibility that's as old as Adam and Eve. Do you remember their excuses in Genesis, Chapter 3? "The serpent beguiled me…it was HIS fault!" and "The woman YOU gave me, God…SHE made me do it!" Him, her, you, them—anybody but ME. That's the blame game, and it's a real growth-stunter. Unsuccessful

> That's the blame game, and it's a real growth-stunter.

people often blame their upbringing, their father's absence, their mother's suffocating presence, their cultural heritage, their fifth grade teacher's cruelty, their hypocritical church, their nation's president, the economy... But the truth is, every man is on his own. The Bible says to, "...work out your salvation with fear and trembling" (Philippians 2:12(b)). Salvation and restoration of the entire life is a process. We are all given a measure of faith, and what we do with it is our own doing.

> Restoration of the entire life is a process.

You can take a tiny acorn and grow an oak from it—and produce a million more acorns over time. Jesus took a kid's lunch and multiplied it to feed 5,000 people. All abundance ever takes is a seed—and God gives us all a seed of faith to plant and take care of. And that seed entails a lot more than religious evangelism. The seed is a hope, a trust, and a reliance on God for all of life. And that is even what evangelism should do—introduce people to the God who wants them to have life, and have it in abundance, now and forever!

> All abundance ever takes is a seed—and God gives us all a seed of faith to plant and take care of.

In John, Chapter 5, there's a story about a crippled man who lay at the Pool of Bethesda, day in and day out. Rumor had it that when an angel came down at random times to stir the waters, the first person to hit the water would be healed. So the man spent all day every day just lying there, waiting for the waters to stir. One day Jesus came by and saw the man lying there, and could tell he'd been there a long time. So Jesus asked him, "Do you want to be made whole?" And the man, instead of answering the question, blamed other people for his situation. First he said, "I have nobody to put me in the pool." And he added, "While I'm struggling, somebody gets there ahead of me!" So first he complains that he has 'nobody', then he complains about the 'somebody' who gets in his way. Nobody, then somebody. Everybody but himself.

Of course, Jesus told the man to get up, take his bed and walk. And surprisingly the man did, and he was made whole. He responded to the help the Lord was offering. He stopped playing the blame game and just did it!

> He stopped playing the blame game and just did it!

Please hear this, Son. To be successful you must be one who takes responsibility for where you are and where you are going. Able-bodied individuals like you and me may have reasons for their state of affairs, but no excuses. Don't let your reasons become excuses on any plane. Don't fall prey to the blame game or spend any time in the moan zone. This is how and where so many people choose to live. Not only does it make for a bummer life emotionally—no growth or achievements will be obtained either. So just remember, nobody owes you. Whatever your life has dealt you, put it behind you and start building! I love what Paul said in 1 Corinthians 16:13, "Be on the alert, stand firm in your faith, act like men, be strong."

> "Be on the alert, stand firm in your faith, act like men, be strong."

Now in your new position with the company you will have a tremendous responsibility. Not only are you responsible for your personal success, but you will also be giving others a launching pad for their own successes. You have hundreds of employees—which means hundreds of families are depending on the success of Montgomery Freight. You are not responsible for how they live their lives, for their wisdom in decision-making, or how they manage their money. But you are responsible to be a good and fair employer. Expect them to do their jobs well, and give them what they need to do it. Don't pinch pennies at their expense. Pay them well and give them good conditions, and you will have a loyal workforce. But you can also teach them to be true to their own responsibilities.

For example, when an employee doesn't pull his/her own weight, there can be consequences that help them learn and achieve—perhaps you can use these principles in the area of bonuses and incentives. Remember I paid for your sister to go to a private Christian college her freshman year? The second year she went to a state school. In semesters two and three her grades fell. I told her if her next semester's grades fell, she would be on her own. Well, they did. And I kept my word, and it was tough. I remember the day she came to this office for money for her fourth semester. I reviewed her grades and reminded her of our previous discussions. I told her she would receive no money. There was no anger involved here, but a principle of responsibility was in play. One lone tear coursed down her cheek to her quivering chin. *"Then Dad, I can't go to college."*

I just told her, *"Sweetie, God will make a way."* I asked her that if our roles were reversed and I was in her place, what would I do?

"You'd find a way," she said.

"Exactly!" I said. *"And so can you! Get to it girl! You can find a way! You can do it!"*

Every fiber in me wanted to bail her out. I hated to see her cry. Candice was always Daddy's little girl. But she had to face the consequences of her behavior or she would never learn. Look at her today—a nurse with a bachelor's degree, a fine husband and a little boy who enjoys a life of prosperity.

Your sister could have quit. That's what most kids in her position would have done. The tendency with human nature is to take the path of least resistance. She could have just found a little job at some fast-food place while waiting for Prince Charming to come and rescue her.

> The tendency with human nature is to take the path of least resistance.

And truly, she might have found a man to care for her. But she would not have realized her own potential, her ability to accept the challenge and overcome her personal obstacles! Too many people in her situation seem to be waiting for the lottery to fix it—or a lawsuit. I even know a lady who gained weight because someone told her she could get on disability if she weighed 300 lbs.! Not surprisingly, that lady died in her 60s. She would still be alive today if she had simply taken responsibility for her life.

I like to get my inspiration from the Bible. And the Old Testament gives a great illustration to help understand the human tendency to shirk responsibility—and how God rewards us when we just take it on!

One of the best-known stories in the Old Testament is the Exodus from Egypt. God sent Moses (played by Charlton Heston in the movie, remember?) to Egypt to lead the Israelites out of slavery. The mission was a spectacular success including many miracles, not the least of which was the parting of the Red Sea. You would think the escapees would have had no trouble trusting such a marvelous God! But it was a mere matter of days before they started to complain about conditions away from slavery. First, the water in the wilderness was undrinkable. They complained about that, accusing Moses of bringing them out to die in the wilderness. Did they not consider that the God who parted the Red Sea could also supply them with water? Despite their lack of faith, God did supply them with clean water. But not long afterward, they complained that there was no food. The land was dry, barren, and seemingly incapable of producing anything edible. Instead of seeking the God of the miraculous, they whined, they murmured. But God was gracious and sent them bread from heaven—every morning the ground was covered with a generous supply of collectible little white bread-flakes that appeared with the morning dew and melted away if it wasn't collected. What was it? They didn't know, so they cleverly named it manna, meaning, "What is it?" Perhaps it was some kind of fungus, like mushrooms that appear overnight. Who knows? But whatever it was, it kept them alive. And it was slightly sweet—I would imagine that bread from heaven must be something akin to

Krispy Kreme donuts! Even if it were, the people got bored with it and complained! They went as far as plotting to kill Moses and go back to Egypt. The trip was just too hard, they thought. Slavery with leeks and onions by the Nile looked better than reaching forward to a fantastic future that was, so far, only a Promise. They couldn't see it, taste it, touch it. And I believe most people choose what they know—even if it's bad—over what they don't know, even if it is much better. People trust their senses more than the intangible, invisible Promises of God. Why? I don't know. Ask Adam and Eve. They started the trend.

> And I believe most people choose what they know—even if it's bad—over what they don't know, even if it is much better.

During Moses' rescue mission, God performed many miracles in order to get Pharaoh to let the Israelites go free. One of the wonders was covering the land of Egypt with frogs. In Exodus, Chapter 8, Moses was summoned by the pharaoh to ask God to end the plague. "If you will remove the frogs you can take the slaves and go." Moses asked the pharaoh when he wanted to be rid of the frogs. Pharaoh answered, "Tomorrow." Tomorrow? Not today? Not right this instant? Basically the pharaoh asked for one more night with the frogs! Perhaps Pharaoh's privileged environs kept himself and his family free from the worst of it. Perhaps he was putting the comfort of his people second to his political meetings and agendas. Any delay is almost too far-fetched to fathom. Yet, I have watched people daily do the same thing. One more night. One more wild party and then I'll stop. One more one-night stand. One more wasteful spending spree. Maybe the frogs of life will just hop away on their own, and the bills will be magically paid with no plan, no work, and no personal responsibility. Hope is not a great strategy.

> Hope is not a great strategy.

Choose now, Son. Choose to grow and become all you can be. Don't wait on the world. It's still blaming and complaining. It's up to you. You can take responsibility for your attitude. Make it one of gratitude. The Exodus story could have been so much better if the attitude and faith of the followers had been better. Yours can be. Take responsibility for your growth; don't just hope it hops away. Like the Israelites who finally made it to the Promised Land, so will you.

This story should jog your memory and help you to see how to take your responsibility and consequences. When you were 12, you asked me to let you drive home from church. You were a pretty good driver—at least, you were great on a lawn mower or golf cart, so I figured, "Why not?" It was a nice sunny day, so when we got to our road we switched spots. We lived out in the country and no one was on the road.

As you started to pick up too much speed for the curves, I warned you to slow down. You were a wild man! You were loving it, and didn't heed my warnings. The third time I took my eyes off the road so I could look at you and emphasize the order to slow down. I can still see every frame of the movie in slow-mo. The road took a curve and you didn't. Since I was looking at you and not the road, I couldn't grab the wheel in time, and we smashed into a telephone and power pole. You never even hit the brakes. I never saw it coming.

Obviously the van came to an abrupt stop! With glass breaking and metal crunching, I never took my eyes off of you. Even when my head cracked the front windshield. *"Mike, are you okay?"* Not a word… Fear gripped me. *"Mike, talk to me!"* One single tear rolled down your cheek. *"I'm sorry, Dad!"*

Fear turned to rage. *"Son, I'm going to kill you! You just totaled Mom's van. She will kill us both!"*

Without exiting the mini-van I could see it was totaled. Both airbags deployed and the front end was gone. *"Well, Son, we are in deep stuff. If we say you were driving, I'm in trouble with the police and the insurance won't pay a penny of this. The cost of the van and pole would be over $20,000. If I say I was driving, no one will know but you and me, and you're going to be cleared. What will we do?"* Your words centered me, brought me back to reality.

"We will tell the truth, Dad."

I was so proud of you. *"You bet we will. I will take responsibility!"* And I did.

I sent you walking home before the police came. I still wavered with the options before me. I wondered, since I was alone maybe he wouldn't ask who was driving. After all, it was just me standing there, with the remains of a deceased vehicle, and a freshly skinned pole in the road. But the first question the officer asked was, of course, *"Were you driving the van, sir?"*

"You mean this van?"

"Yes, sir. Were you driving?"

"No, sir."

"Who was?"

"My son, and he went home. We just live one block away and were almost home."

"Sir, it's illegal to leave the scene of an accident."

"I know; he doesn't have his license."

"How old is he?"

It was at that point that I saw the absurdity of the incident.

"Excuse me? How old is your son?"

My voice lost over half its strength. *"Twelve,"* I managed to scratch out.

"Excuse me?"

"HE'S TWELVE!"

"Are you an idiot?"

"Yes sir, I am. Guilty as charged."

"I've been a sheriff's deputy for 16 years, and I have never seen anything like this."

"Yes sir, you have. Everybody else lied to you."

The officer knew I was telling the truth. The easy way out. What would I have taught you, Son? What would God have thought? He always knows the truth. I could have blamed you. I could have lied. It wasn't my fault. I can hear the cry of our culture, "IT'S NOT MY FAULT! As long as it's not my fault, I need to do nothing! Someone will fix it for me!" No, Son, that's the way to bondage! Truth will always make you free in the long run. Do the right thing, every time. The accident was my fault. First, I broke the law by letting you drive. I was supposed to be the adult. Ha! I also should have been watching the road. I could have grabbed the wheel; could have taken the curve you skipped. It was my fault. And I owned up to it in court.

> As long as it's not my fault, I need to do nothing!

After the deputy got over his shock about your driving, he let me know I was in trouble. He actually debated arresting me and even called his sergeant to help in deciding what to do with me.

The deputy chilled out some, and told me to drop by the station. I was relieved. He said it was a formality and no big deal. On the appointed day, I showed up on time—shaved, showered and in a new suit. Every little bit helps. I was taken back behind bars. This made me a little nervous. Then I was seated with three "criminals" waiting to be processed. At the time I didn't recognize what was happening to me.

Somehow things were not looking good. I comforted myself with the "arresting" officer's words. "No big deal." But the next step in this hit parade was fingerprinting. Mine! Now I was officially nervous. This was starting to feel like a big deal. I was processed with the rest of the criminals. At the last stop I was assigned a court date. I looked at the officer with a puzzled face. *"Sir, the deputy who gave me the ticket told me this was not a big deal!"* The officer in charge peered at me over the top of his bifocals and said, *"Mr. Montgomery, you have been charged with a felony. Reckless endangerment of a minor."*

Son, it was at that point I wanted to tell him how you had put me in danger! But he didn't seem to have a sense of humor, so I let that thought go! *"Sir, your charge carries with it a mandatory one year sentence and a $20,000 fine."* Suddenly all the humor drained from my head as the blood drained from my face. Guess he got the last laugh. I was speechless! *"If I were you, I'd find me a good lawyer."* I should have seen a bad thing brewing when they seated me with the hardened criminals in their orange prison suits and heavy chains.

I tried to call the deputy. When I reached him, he told me he wasn't supposed to speak to me. *"What? But you said not to worry, no big deal!"* I was in deep weeds. I called everyone I knew to try to get some help but none came. I kept panicking, thinking, I can't go to jail! As the court date drew closer the more concerned I became. The day finally dawned. I had not been in trouble since 1980-something, B.C.—my years Before Christ. The drug days. The judge looked me up and down. I tried my best to look out of place. And I was hoping I didn't just get Judge Judy's brother.

"Mr. Montgomery, it sounds like you've been through quite an ordeal!"

"Yes, sir," was all I had time to say.

The gavel dropped and he decreed, *"Case dismissed!"*

"Excuse me, Your Hon—?"

"Case dismissed. You're free to go."

I was floored. Ecstatic, but I could barely stand! That judgment was sheer grace! I did NOT get what I deserved. But God blessed me. Whether he blessed me because I told the truth, I guess I'll know someday (perhaps I know today, as you're watching this DVD!). The Lord has no obligation to get the guilty off the hook down here. But He did. And I was so glad I had told the truth. Acquiring freedom under false pretenses would have been a long-term sentence of self-imposed misery. Taking responsibility imparted its own sense of freedom. And grace—I did not deserve such grace! But grace is what we get when we put our trust in Jesus for salvation and forgiveness. Under such grace, we are surprised over and over! Just like I danced out of the hospital at 22 years of age, I danced out of the courtroom as a free and forgiven man. It sure felt good! Grace—yes, how sweet the sound!

> I did NOT get what I deserved.

> Acquiring freedom under false pretenses would have been a long-term sentence of self-imposed misery.

I Don't Have Time

DAD CONTINUED:

Growing up, Son, we heard a stockpile of sermons on stewardship, or money management. Most church members seemed to blow those sermons off as just the church wanting additional funds. For some reason that I can only attribute to God, I listened. Every message on being a manager—that is what a steward is—impacted me all the more. As I listened and applied the lesson, I realized I really owned nothing. God owned it all. Everything I had or was, was a gift from God for me to use as freely as I pleased. All talents, abilities, money or possessions were for Him. They were on loan, and one day I would give an accounting of how I used or invested them. Even you, Son, were a loan from God. It was my responsibility to disciple you, to prepare you to be used by Him. This lesson should change your entire perspective of life.

Again, many church members think of stewardship as giving 10 percent of one's income—the tithe—to the Lord, through the church. To be sure, that is essential, but it is only the beginning. You, Son, will also be held accountable to God for how you spent, blew or invested your time. Right now you have a finite number of days, minutes and seconds to live. Look at your watch. The second hand is ticking off moments, ever nearing that end. You can't add one second to the timetable God set. So, Son, how will you spend it?

If you pray, plan and prepare your personal growth plan, much of your time will be planned. You will be able to prioritize your time as to what is most important. Far too many people pick up their calendar and start there, working on time, but that is the wrong place to start. Start by listing your priorities. Use the Five F's I already listed for you.

> If you pray, plan and prepare your personal growth plan, much of your time will be planned.

Once you set your priorities, then get them on paper. Get a daily planner and learn to write things down. If you don't set your priorities and agenda, someone else will do it for you. Probably they won't set your time according to your priorities. Who else has your priorities and your best interest at heart? Take charge of and responsibility for how you spend your time. Review your growth plans and priorities often. Check them against your calendar to ensure you don't drift off course. Getting off course is so easy. It requires no effort at all.

> Getting off course is so easy. It requires no effort at all.

When we lived in Southwest Louisiana I used to go spear fishing about 30-50 miles off shore. I took you with me until you started getting seasick. One Saturday we had loaded the boat with red snapper and amberjack. We were on the way back when my friend who owned the boat asked me to pilot. You remember Dr. Chip? He usually did all the skippering but this day he was tired and wanted to catch a nap. He told me to hold steady at 15 degrees and we'd be fine. About an hour later he woke up to find that we were way off course! I took up for myself, pointing out that I had kept it steady at about 15 degrees.

"About? About 15 degrees?" he said indignantly. "Just one degree off

> Just one degree off course for 60 minutes and you are pretty far off. Do you know how far off we are?

course for 60 minutes and you are pretty far off. Do you know how far off we are?"

"Nope." I hadn't done well in geometry—I failed triangles. But I could tell we were many miles away from where we should have been, and our trip home was going to be a bit longer than planned.

"Well, let me put it to you this way; you don't get to drive again!" He said, laughing at me. I never lived that one down!

Son, what an important life lesson to learn; just one degree off for a while and you have missed the mark by miles.

> Son, what an important life lesson to learn; just one degree off for a while and you have missed the mark by miles.

This same thing will happen to your calendar and priorities if not protected diligently. You must continually be careful how you spend time. People, hobbies, issues and who knows what will always be pulling at you. Resist the "tyranny of the urgent" by choosing in advance how your time will be spent. Don't let others' poor planning pull you off course. If you have planned and prioritized your time, you will have most calendaring questions answered before others ask. Don't leave it up to chance. Chance or choice—which one do you think will pay off?

Now as far as your personal growth plan goes, don't fall into the common time traps. When I talk to people about a growth plan, the answer is the same: "I don't have time!" We all have 24 hours a day, Son, no more and no less! No one ever found 20 minutes lying on the

> "Make the most of your time."

sidewalk! That is definitely not how to discover time. With some clever calculating you can maximize your time. The Bible says, "Make the most of your time" (Ephesians 5:16(a), paraphrased). You'll probably need to spend a little time dealing with what you need to drop from your schedule or priority list. Adding to your calendar requires dropping other things.

Now let's get creative, Son. Look at the things on your growth plan. If you don't have your plan written down, you probably don't have one. In the envelope are some sheets that will help get you going. As I list my ideas for you, your creative juices will begin to flow, so write down all your ideas so you can test-drive them.

The first thing I did after I had a growth plan was to enroll in Automotive University. I don't mean an automotive repair class; I mean growth time in the car. The average American who lives to be eighty years old will spend five full years of 24-hour days in the car. That's a lot of time. It takes much less time to complete college—one year's worth of 24-hour days. A person could earn a degree!

Think of five full years enrolled in Automotive University and how you could maximize your time. In my current growth plan I have as a goal to read 52 books this year. That's one per week. So, getting good books on CD can make drives in the car great. Another part of my plan is to memorize 52 verses. See a pattern? So, I put Bible verse cards in my car. At red lights, stop

> Why should the devil get all the use out of technology?

signs or in traffic jams, I can review current cards or work on my next memory verse. Another part of my plan is to listen to two leadership lessons each month. So, I get these on CDs. I can listen on the road or download them to my iPod. (Why should the devil get all the use out of technology?) Son, this is called multi-tasking. You are much too smart not to use your time wisely. You'll think of many more ways to make your time count.

"But, I don't have the time." This is nothing more than an excuse for those who don't really want to in the first place. We all make time for what we really want. You can use the time in the car to mentor your kids if you ever have them. I know you remember the many talks we had in the car. Psalm 139:16 says, "Your eyes have seen my unformed substance; and in Your book were written all the days that were ordained for me when as yet there was not one of them."

When people think of the term stewardship, it is automatically money. You, Son, will one day give an account to God for how you spent all the time He gave you. This is much bigger than money. You can always get more money; but time spent can never be recovered or redeemed. Please hear this, Son.

> You still have some to spend. Spend them well.

It's too important to miss. Every second counts. Think about it. You and I will never spend another second together here on earth. That pains me. If you're watching this, it means I have spent all my seconds, and I have no more. You still have some to spend. Spend them well.

Time in your car can be maximized and family time can be experienced if you will turn off the CDs and DVDs. Your mom and I had great talks while traveling. When you guys were young we played games and made up songs and had crazy family times together! You can be as creative as you like—just spend lots of time interacting with one another.

Now that you are grown, keep a book in the car and if you arrive to your appointments early, grab a few pages.

If you want to grow, you have all the time you need if it's a priority. A person makes time for the things he wants to accomplish. For instance, this DVD—it was something I wanted you to have. I hoped maybe someday it would be treasured by my grandkids. I had vision for it. And that drive enabled me to make time to prepare it. I couldn't really know whether it was urgent, since I didn't know for sure whether I was going to die soon. I could have easily put it off, gambling on the chance that I might live 20 more years. But my desire to do it compelled me to find the time. I came to work an hour early and spent my lunch times planning each lesson. I asked our technical crew to set up a camera in my office where all I had to do was push the record button.

I approach my entire personal growth plan with that same kind of anticipation, Son, and I hope you can relate to that personally. I wanted to be the best I could be for the Lord. So, daily I enjoyed the spiritual disciplines. "Be diligent to present yourself approved to God as a workman who does not need to be ashamed..." (2 Timothy 2:15). Daily I asked the Lord to transform me. Remember it's a process, not a one-time event. I so longed to be a tool God could use. I prayed often I would be on the top shelf of God's toolbox. When God needed someone to use, I would be ready! Does this make sense to you? I wanted to be like a power tool, clean, greased and ready for Him to use. Personal growth has been a delight, not a duty. For me it's been a passion, not a pastime.

> Personal growth has been a delight, not a duty. For me it's been a passion, not a pastime.

Try to make time work for you, not against you. You need recreation time, but you can't schedule it so tightly that it just feels like another obligation. Remember when we bought that 1956 Corvette? You, Zeke and I were going to make a hot rod out of it. Then we decided to put it back perfectly stock. At first the project was fun. But we were also in the final stages of building house #3. At that point we ran out of money for the house. We needed to finish the car so we could sell it and complete the house. That made a fun project turn into grueling work. What was meant as a project for us turned into a job. Why? Time. A great hobby was preempted by working a deadline. It turned out beautifully, but not with the memories I had planned. Learn off my dime again. Make time your ally, not your enemy.

> Make time your ally, not your enemy.

Son, I so hope and pray you see it the same way. God has big plans for you. He requires that we be ready. If you will be teachable, moldable, humble and willing, He will take you far beyond your dreams. "…And what does the Lord require of you but to do justice, to love kindness, and to walk humbly with your God?" (Micah 6:8)

———————————

Dad had that twinkle in his eye again. It looked like a tear, but it was just love. Just love? How can I put it in such trite terms? Real love is so rare, so priceless, and it was so plentiful in him! How I had taken it for granted!

I paused the computer again, just to stare at the love… After a moment or so, I looked around the room. It was late in the evening. The sun had already set and the room had grown dark. The day had passed by so quickly, I had not even noticed. I thought of the treasure this day had been, yet it was gone in the blink of an eye. How many days could I have filled with treasure like this one? How many days slipped by, never to be again? They were gone, like Dad—gone without my full attention, swallowed without tasting. If I had known my time with Dad was so short, I would have reordered my life. I would have spent more time with him. He kept trying to schedule time in the mountains at some river cabin… I always had an exam, or a date, or something. I guess none of us know how much time we have. That's what he was trying to tell me—that none of us knows. Why should we suffer through a precious day and call it mundane? Why should we ever find a moment of boredom? What a joke, to complain that there's nothing to do! So many times I had wished away the present. Tears burned my eyes again, and I just let them flow.

> How many days could I have filled with treasure like this one? How many days slipped by, never to be again?

Ch.13

What If I Hit the Wall?

DAD CONTINUED:

Well, Son, one of the most difficult things about preparing this DVD for you was the realization that I will not ever be there to help you or our family again. Our years together have been awesome and we have all grown. Our family has always helped each other. Now you will be on your own. Without question you will hit the wall from time to time. By the wall, I mean you will discover areas of your life where you're deficient. If they are not removed, they will keep you from moving forward. What will you do?

Hitting the wall happens to us all. Surprisingly, few ever get over that wall. This has been another enigma for me. To just keep doing what you

> Hitting the wall happens to us all.

have always done and expect different results—insanity! But, Son, this is how the masses march. They move through life without thought of overcoming or growing past the wall. Sad! This is one of the reasons the divorce, bankruptcy, addiction and suicide rates continue to rise. People without hope for the future have no power in the present. It can always get better. The Bible is full of miracles and accounts of men

> People without hope for the future have no power in the present.

and women who overcame their obstacles! Be one of the overcomers! 1 Corinthians 13:11 says, "When I was a child, I used to speak like a child, think like a child, reason like a child; when I became a man, I did away with childish things." Follow suit, Son.

Your Personal Growth Plan should change or be adjusted with time. It's like a training plan at a health club—your trainer will adjust your regimen as you grow in strength and endurance. As one grows stronger, the plan needs to be adjusted to accommodate increasing skill and ability. The same thing happens when there's an injury in training. The plan is adjusted to accommodate it for a while. It is the same with your Personal Growth Plan. It's a living document, not a legalistic decree! So, when you hit the wall, your plan will have to be adjusted.

Step one is to identify the wall. Please don't ignore it like so many do. It could be in any of the Five F's—the areas of major importance: Faith, Family, Fitness, Fortune and Future. Once you've pinpointed the problem, the next step is finding someone to help. As much as possible, stay within the family of God. I say this in order to keep your solutions within the framework of values that create success. You see, if you and your wife encounter problems in your relationship, you may do well to seek a counselor. But as you do, you need to realize that there are counselors out there who do not value the idea of Covenant the way God does, and therefore may not seek to preserve it. Instead, they may seek to merely preserve individual happiness, which is fleeting and fickle. And by simply ridding yourselves of one another, you would miss the deep joy that comes through restoration. So while you try to find the best helpers in the field, evaluate

> The bottom line is to get godly help.

what "best" really is. It could be a faithful old counselor of some years; or it could be a mentor from afar, someone you might not even know, someone with books or CDs on the subject. The Lord will direct you if you acknowledge Him in this. The bottom line is to get godly help.

Your Personal Growth Plan should show your plan and progress as you overcome the wall. Never settle for stagnancy in your development toward your personal potential. Walls can be climbed over, around or under. There is always a way through. And the Lord will lead you there.

Early in my career with the company, I hit the wall. The company had grown rapidly, but it was growing faster than I was. The growth forced me to hire more staff and expand departments. Operational changes were also necessitated. Son, I wasn't prepared or equipped. I didn't know how to handle it. I felt like you must feel today. I had gained my academic degree and certificates and had attended so many seminars, yet I was in way over my head. I knew I lacked leadership, so I went after some help.

I thought about going back to school, of course. But after a few conversations with highbrow, tenured professors, I realized they didn't share my passion for personal growth beyond the nuts and bolts of bean counting. I needed practical help.

> I needed practical help.

I was praying for help when a spiritual mentor, John Yarbrough, popped into the picture. Remember the pastor who helped me? John was that pastor. He told me he had signed up for a "tape of the month" club. I realize the word "tape" dates me. But, boy was it the mentor from afar that I required! It was the INJOY Life Club by Dr. John Maxwell. Later Maxwell became the number one author on leadership in the country.

The leadership lessons enabled me to go to the next level. I bought every book and tape he had done. For years my personal growth plan reflected the "wall" of leadership. I developed and processed the information and put the lessons into my life. The growth was steady and gradual. Daily disciplines are essential.

Mentors from afar are people you will rarely meet. Yet, miracles do occur. After two years of reading and listening to John Maxwell, I went to one of his conferences. I was excited to get to meet the person who had contributed so much to my growth. We hit it off and even had a meal together. John saw my hunger to grow as a leader and poured into my life. I met with him several times in the ensuing years, and he gave me much additional material. In 1996 he invited your mom and me to his house for the weekend. Wow!

The weekend was filled with fun and growth. At the end of the weekend, I asked John and his wife, Margaret, to pray for your mom and me. Wow, it was a great experience, and I felt the Lord imparted something to us that day. We left there inspired, encouraged and motivated.

You have experienced the same thing as a little boy. When you were about nine years old, you hit the wall. It was a wall of fear. You were just a little guy, but fear and gloom gripped you like a vise, and it took me a bit of time to realize what was happening to you. We were preparing to leave Louisiana and move to Knoxville. I was hiring an employee in Louisiana. That sweet lady told me a story that I thought was rather bizarre, but the Lord was planting a seed of awareness in my busy brain. This woman said that when she was your age her family moved to southwest Louisiana and that she was overcome with fear after the move. She said she would go into her parents' room at night to see if they were still breathing. She was afraid they would die and she would be alone. The move had rattled her world to the point that she developed a serious sense of insecurity.

I thought that even though she was a little girl, her response to change was rather silly. But that same week we told you we were moving. I didn't see your fear right away, but you were overcome with it. Your little mind was so troubled. For the next three years you were fearful of everything. Your mother and I were so perplexed—we didn't have a clue how to handle such an issue.

But God did. One day a pastor friend of mine, and his wife, stopped in Knoxville for a visit. Remember Dennis Watson? He was well versed in "warfare prayer." While they were at our house he basically cast a spirit of fear right out of you! Your life was transformed because, by the grace and power of God, you overcame the wall. You were a new boy! Every obstacle in life can be overcome by the power of God, whether by casting out spirits or working through issues the usual way. But it's the same power, the same God, who gives you understanding, opportunities, even miraculous circumstances that will enable you to overcome every hindering force!

> Every obstacle in life can be overcome by the power of God.

Son, never allow a wall to hinder you from your potential. Let the multitude stop and hit the wall—you soar to the next level. Walls are there for you to grow beyond. Mountains are there to be climbed. You can also enjoy the journey. Find someone ahead of you for help.

Help, I've Fallen and I Can't Get Up!

DAD CONTINUED:

Well, I bet after hours of watching, listening and learning, you probably still feel somewhat alone! Maybe confused and even overwhelmed. It's kind of like the old commercial everybody made fun of until it happened to them: "Help, I've fallen and I can't get up!" Many times I have felt the same way. I don't mean lying on the floor, but all alone. Once you set a course to become all you can be, you can feel like you've left some people behind. Many have made the choice not to take the cruise. They have said "no" to the train of personal growth and change. Stagnation becomes their situation; familiarity their friend.

> Many have made the choice not to take the cruise. They have said "no" to the train of personal growth and change. Stagnation becomes their situation; familiarity their friend.

God never intended life to be a solo sport. Life is a team event. You can go all the way back to the beginning. In Genesis, right at the start of life, God said, "It is not good for man to be alone" (Genesis 2:18). God intended for us to live in community with each other. Others can help make the journey a joy. Make sure and pick the people who will take the ride with you. If you choose wisely they will lift you, or poorly and they will limit you.

I have been blessed with so many friends in this life. Several stick out as stellar. One friend I had for well over half of my life was Chet. You kids all called him Uncle Chet. There really hasn't been a major event in life that he missed. He was even there when you were born.

At one particularly low point, Chet came to the rescue. It was right after I finished college. Everything in life seemed to come unraveled. I had not landed a job. I got very sick, and the engine blew up in our minivan. That was our only means of transportation. Chet took my van and had the engine rebuilt. I was clueless. He picked up the whole tab—$2,000. That was a lot of money in 1989. But that was the kind of friend Chet was. You could call him today and he would be there for you, just like he was for me.

I remember one day he called to ask me to pray for his mom. He told me not to make the two-hour drive to the hospital in Chattanooga. He was not sure how serious it was. Your mom told me she had a bad feeling, and that I should go on to visit Chet. I have learned to listen to your mom's feelings. I got in the car and headed to the hospital. As soon as I got to the room, Chet walked out the door and into my arms. His mom

> That's what friends do; we hold each other's arms up. We do all we can do to lift them to the next level.

had just died. I could feel his loss as we embraced, and he could feel my love. That's what friends do; we hold each other's arms up. We do all we can do to lift them to the next level. Even if we have to hoist them up using our hands as their stirrups. No one can do it alone.

Moses was one of the greatest leaders of history. Over 3,500 years later, his fame is renowned. If you read the story closely you'll see that even at the Burning Bush God gave him a friend to travel with him and help. His partner's name was Aaron—his brother.

Later in the narrative we find Moses and the Israelites in a life and death battle. Moses went to the mountaintop to pray for the army. In Exodus 17:11-12 we learn that when Moses held his hands up they would begin to win. When his hands would drop the enemy gained the advantage. So, Aaron and a friend named Hur pulled up a rock for Moses to sit on. They also got on either side and held up his arms until Israel won. Son, you must have people who will hold up your hands; so many in this company have done that for me.

Part of holding up someone's hands is holding each other accountable. A personal growth plan makes accountability easy. Once you have developed this plan, give it to one or two close, trusted friends. Meet weekly for breakfast or coffee to see how your week compares to the plan you completed. You can pray for each other daily, keeping in mind your partner's plan. A growth plan is a tool that makes mutual accountability accessible to anyone who will put forth the effort. Not easy.

> A personal growth plan makes accountability easy.

Let's go back to the health club illustration we talked about before. If you get someone to work out with you, your chance of continuing will double. Mutual accountability helps both parties achieve the desired goal. We really are better together because that's how God designed us.

> If you get someone to work out with you, your chance of continuing will double.

Please pick your partners with caution. They will have more to do with how far you go than you know. Who's got your back? Who's pushing you to pursue your potential? Who's cheering you on? Who is thrilled with your victories? With whom can you share the ride? Ecclesiastes 4:9-12 tells us, "Two are better than one because they have a good return for their labor. For if either of them falls, the one will lift up his companion. But woe to the one who falls when there is not another to lift him up. Furthermore, if two lie down together they keep warm, but how can one be warm alone? And if one can overpower him who is alone, two can resist him. A cord of three strands is not quickly torn apart."

It is so much more fun to grow and achieve together. It would be like playing golf alone and making a hole-in-one. With whom would you share, celebrate and retell the story? Into whose hand can you hand your Personal Growth Plan? Do they care to keep you on track?

"Help, I've fallen and I can't get up!" is a scary thought. Actually, it's a matter of life or death. Someone alone and down will die without help. Son, who are you helping? Who would help you? One person in this company you can count on is Josh. Our company has more than doubled since he became president. I trust him explicitly. He will watch out for you. He has been a trusted friend. Surround yourself with men like this and be a great friend.

Since the journey is not an easy one, it only goes to reason many will bail when trials come. Never let it cause you to quit. Hebrews 12:1 says, "Therefore, since we have so great a cloud of witnesses surrounding us, let us also lay aside every encumbrance and the sin which so easily entangles us, and let us run with endurance the race that is set before us." As you run your race to your potential, think of me in the stands cheering you on. I am and will be proud of you. Remember this when it gets hard, Son.

> As you run your race to your potential, think of me in the stands cheering you on. I am and will be proud of you. Remember this when it gets hard, Son.

Who's Going to Pick Up the Tab?

DAD CONTINUED:

Well, Son, it's not easy for me, but I have to land this plane. One good thing about this is that you can watch this DVD again. There's another copy in your mother's safe deposit box at the bank, for safekeeping. I can only imagine how shocking today must be for you. I bet the last days have all been pretty tough, but so are you—tough, that is. All your life I have tried to add steel to your spine.

> All your life I have tried to add steel to your spine.

Soon life will move back into some kind of normalcy. It will never be like it was, but it's not supposed to be. God's mercies are new every morning because the demands of each day are new. My goal was not to pull together a lifetime of teaching in one day, but to remind you of the lifetime of teaching you have received. I wanted this to be both informative and inspirational to encourage you towards a life of personal growth by developing and maintaining a plan. Let me leave you with one more motivation to maintain. This thought has helped push me through some very hard times. I want this imagery to be imprinted on your mind as it has been on mine.

The Scripture is what my life has been built on. It is very plain truth in the Bible that we are stewards and we will be held accountable. Romans 14:12 leaves little room for interpretation: "So, then each one of us will give an account of himself to God." It is hard to skate around a day of reckoning. You and I both will give an account of how well we lived and used all God has given us. Your time, talents and treasure will all be open for scrutiny. If you reread the four Gospels you

> "So, then each one of us will give an account of himself to God."

will find a pile of parables dealing with our accounting. It was one of Jesus' main topics. "And there is no creature hidden from His sight, but all things are open and laid bare to the eyes of Him whom we have to do" (Hebrews 4:13).

Mike, I have tried to live daily with this day in mind. I have tried to prepare you for this accounting. There should be very few things more paramount in your priorities. Let me be very clear and concise. This accounting is not about your sin. Your sin was judged and paid for at the cross. When you gave your heart to Jesus, your sins were forgiven and thrown away. Every sin you would ever commit is covered by the blood of Jesus shed on the cross. This concept is also very clear in Scripture.

Now, back to the day of accounting. Your "works" will be judged—how you lived your life compared to the gifts God has given you. All this stacked against the potential He poured into you. This is what the apostle said about it in 2 Corinthians 5:9-11, "Therefore we also have as our ambition, whether at home or absent, to be pleasing to Him. For we must all appear before the judgment seat of Christ so that each one may be recompensed for his deeds in the body, according to what he has done,

> Your "works" will be judged—how you lived your life compared to the gifts God has given you. All this stacked against the potential He poured into you.

whether good or bad. Therefore knowing the fear of the Lord we persuade men..."

Don't be confused about "judgment" and "recompense." People naturally think God is going to stand there with a big stick, ready to knock you into hell for all of your shortcomings—and we all have shortcomings. But God has wonderful things to bestow upon His children! We don't know what heaven will be like, but I think we can assume that what we learn here will help us comprehend a few things there—and that, in itself, will constitute reward. But there's far more, as it is written: "No eye has seen, no ear has heard, no mind has conceived what God has prepared for those who love Him" (1 Corinthians 2:9, paraphrased). What a wonderful motivation!

Son, this is so much more important than you can possibly realize. So many cruise past this in today's culture because you live in a society where few take responsibility for their actions. Our society excuses just about every possible situation. It is the atmosphere that permeates our homes, hearts and churches. It is hard to conceive standing and giving an account in this culture. Beware, Son, of taking your cues from culture. Without any effort on your part, the culture will allow you to coast away from Christ. I could list many more statements from Scripture to prove my point. I don't need to because you know this to be true. This teaching flows straight from the Savior's heart.

> It is hard to conceive standing and giving an account in this culture.

I so want to prepare you to stand at the judgment seat and hear these words: "Well done, my good and faithful servant. Enter into the joy of your Master" (Matthew 25:21, paraphrased). Even as I quote these words looking into the camera, my heart longs for you to be ready! Son, this is why a growth plan, goals, daily disciplines and prioritizing your life is so essential. Your life here on earth will be short, I know. Your time in Heaven will last forever.

You know how much I love the Apostle Paul. He penned 13 of the letters in the New Testament. I can almost feel his heart as he writes and seeks to please the Lord. One of my favorite verses comes from his last letter that bears Timothy's name. It was his second letter to Timothy, his son in the ministry. Paul was a prisoner as he wrote the letter. He was awaiting execution. Death row for no crime is not a peaceful place for most. He could probably hear the executioner sharpening the axe to remove his head. Paul lived his whole Christian life for the judgment seat. He had a healthy fear of the day. Listen to his last paragraph to his beloved son in 2 Timothy 4:6-8, "…the time of my departure has come. I have fought the good fight, I have finished the course, I have kept the faith; in the future there is laid up for me the crown of righteousness, which the Lord, the righteous Judge, will award to me on that day; and not only to me, but to all who have loved His appearing."

As I read his words I can feel his heart and his relief. He didn't blow it. He was ready for the day of accounting. He had been faithful and fruitful. Are you? I will be there when you are judged. I so long to see you rewarded by our Lord and hear the words, "Well done." From the day you were born, I dedicated you to the Lord. I devoted time to

> He was ready for the day of accounting.

help prepare and disciple you. I have seen great gifts and abilities erupt from your life. I believe God has big plans for you. "To whom much is given, much is required" (Luke 12:48, paraphrased). I believe Jesus was serious when He spoke those words. Now, 21 centuries later they still ring as true as when He spoke them. I believe they apply to you.

One day you will be here with me. Together we will walk the streets of gold. I look forward to your arrival here in Heaven. But until that day, give God your best, "…knowing that your toil is not in vain in the Lord" (1 Corinthians 15:58).

One last thing. Remember when we lived in Louisiana and I was gone on a trip? You were probably eight or nine years old. I left you in charge as usual. That evening you guys couldn't get to the house because a snake was blocking the sidewalk. Your mom wouldn't let you go to get one of my guns to kill it. She was afraid you were too young. And I guess you were, at that. But Son, now you're the man. Take up the weapons of the warfare—they're not carnal or earthly. They're mighty through God, and will enable you to pull down the strongholds that seek to keep each of you captive in your respective prisons of fear, doubt, and unbelief—the enemies of joy! Take your ground, Mike! Trust the Holy Spirit to guide your life; I now trust my family into your capable hands.

> Take up the weapons of the warfare.

And although earth never renders enough time, someday we'll be able to sit down for a long time and do nothing but enjoy our life stories in the Presence of the Savior, who was there with us, too! Meanwhile, take care of your mom. She is valuable and precious. Treat her like a queen for me! By the way, she loves jewelry at Christmas—and make over all her holiday doo-dads. She loves it! Savor the moments, and keep our family together.

Until I see you here…soar!

———————————

Dad had that awesome smile on his face—and the twinkle in his eye! The scene dissolved into film footage of me, flying over the water near Virginia Beach. I was hanging from a glider being towed by a boat. I was way up there, but my smile was unmistakable. What people below couldn't see was why. I was free. Free from fear. God had set me free, and I was free indeed. I know Dad used that clip to remind me that I can do it.

I turned off the DVD player. It was 12:31 a.m. A new day had begun. And as I flipped off the lights and closed the door behind me, I knew I'd be back real soon. I knew that with God's help, I could do anything I set my mind to do. I could run this company; I could lose

> A new day had begun.

the extra weight; I could have a family; and I could glorify God with a life well lived. <u>Yes, I was a man with a Plan.</u>

The CD on the front cover contains all the worksheets from the Appendix as printable PDF files.

Personal Growth Plan for: _____

The number one command in the canon of the Bible is: *"To love the Lord your God with all your heart, soul, strength, and all your mind" (Deuteronomy 6:5, paraphrased).* That sounds like a lot of effort. The purpose of this plan is to help you accomplish God's heart and your desire; to obey the first commandment.

> Jude 20-21: *"But you beloved, building yourself up on your most holy faith, praying in the Holy Spirit. Keep yourselves in the love of God, waiting anxiously for the mercy of our Lord Jesus Christ to eternal life."*

Quantify the spiritual disciplines below so you can measure them. They can be measured by differing amounts of time or pages.

BIBLE READING: _____ (pages or chapters–daily or annually)

> Psalm 19:7-8: *"The Law of the Lord is perfect, restoring the soul; the testimony of the Lord is sure, making wise the simple. The precepts of the Lord are right, rejoicing the heart; the commandment of the Lord is pure, enlightening the eyes."*

My recommendation is to read the entire Bible annually.

Options: Read straight through, Bible reading record, Chronological Bible, One-Year Bible. (Straight-through reading is not recommended for the novice, as it is easy to get bogged down in some of the Old Testament.)

BIBLE STUDY: _____ (amount of time, topics, books to be studied, studies)

> 2 Timothy 2:15; 3:16-17: *"Be diligent to present yourself approved to God as a workman who does not need to be ashamed, accurately handling the Word of truth …" "All Scripture is inspired by God and profitable for teaching, for reproof, for correction, for training in righteousness; so that the man of God may be adequate, equipped for every good work."*

You may choose topics of interest, character studies, book studies, word studies, Small Group Bible studies, prepared studies, e.g., Beth Moore, Precepts, etc.

SCRIPTURE MEMORY: _____ (# of verses annually)

> Psalm 119:11: *"Your Word have I treasured in my heart, that I might not sin against you."*

Use areas of growth you need: evangelism verses, prayer promises, faith. (I would suggest the "Roman Road" to salvation–Romans 3:10; 3:23; 5:8; 6:23; 10:9-10; 13)

MEDITATION: _____ (amount of time)

> Psalm 104:34; 119:97-99: *"Let my meditation be pleasing to Him; as for me I shall be glad in the Lord." "O how I love Your law! It is my meditation all the day. Your commandments make me wiser than my enemies, for they are ever mine. I have more insight than all my teachers, for Your testimonies are my meditation."*

Daily in the Scriptures, names of God, doctrines, attributes of God, memory verses, etc.

SILENCE: _____ (amount of time)

> Psalm 46:10; 62:5: *"Cease striving and know that I am God; I will be exalted among the nations, I will be exalted in all the earth." "My soul, wait in silence for God only, for my hope is from Him."*

Structured listening to God, listening to the Holy Spirit, discerning the Will of God, reflecting on issues, reflecting on events, reflecting on your day, problems, or the future.

SOLITUDE: _____ (amount of time)

> Psalm 27:5; 31:20: *"For in the day of trouble He will conceal me in His tabernacle; in the secret place of His tent he will hide me; He will lift me up on a rock." "You hide them in the secret place of Your presence from the conspiracies of man; You keep them secretly in a shelter from the strife of tongues."*

When, where, rest, bask in His presence and His glory, receive His power.

PRAYER: _____ (specific amount of time)

> I Samuel 12:23; I Thessalonians 5:17: *"Moreover, as for me, far be it from me that I should sin against the Lord by ceasing to pray for you; but I will instruct you in the good and right way." "Pray without ceasing."*

Create a list of family, friends, coworkers, spiritual leaders, political leaders, church family, harvest of souls, revival, ministries, missionaries, etc.

FASTING: _____ (# of meals, days, seasons)

> Matthew 6:16: *"Whenever you fast, do not put on a gloomy face as the hypocrites do, for they neglect their appearance so that they will be noticed by men when they are fasting, Truly I say to you, they have their reward in full."*

I would recommend starting with one meal and working your way up to one full day, three days, seven days, and longer. Plan for prayer times during the fast. Study Isaiah 58 in preparation.

EVANGELISM: _____ (# of people you will share the Gospel with this year)

Acts 1:8: *"But you will receive power when the Holy Spirit has come upon you; and you shall be My witnesses both in Jerusalem, and in all Judea and Samaria, and even to the remotest part of the earth."*

Create a list of people to pray for and share with:

FAMILY   FRIENDS   CO-WORKERS

_____   _____   _____

_____   _____   _____

_____   _____   _____

BOOKS READ: _____ (# of books for the year)

Consider topics, areas of interest or growth, areas of strengths or weaknesses. (I recommend one out of every ten books be a positive attitude book, areas of professional proficiency, areas to stretch you)

CDs, DVDs, PODCASTS, BLOGS: _____ (# listened to)

Proverbs 4:23: *"Watch over your heart with all diligence, for from it flow the springs of life."*

Leadership, sermons, worship. (Enroll in U. of A. - University of Automobile by making the best use of time in the car and travel!)

SERVING: _____ (amount of time)

John 13:14-15; I Peter 4:10: *"If I then, the Lord and the Teacher, washed your feet, you also ought to wash one another's feet. For I gave you an example that you also should do as I did to you." "As each one has received a special gift, employ it in serving one another as good stewards of the manifold grace of God."*

Inside the church, out in the community, with the poor, visiting jail or prison, areas to which you feel called.

MISSION TRIPS: _____ (Annual trips? When do you plan to go?)

Matthew 28:19-20: *"Go therefore and make disciples of all the nations, baptizing them in the name of the Father and the Son and the Holy Spirit, teaching them to observe all that I commanded you; and lo, I am with you always, even to the end of the age."*

List Areas In Your Spiritual Walk That Need Improvement:

_____

_____

_____

Your personal plan should reflect all of the disciplines and the areas in which you want to grow.

"Your life is like a vapor, here today and gone tomorrow." ~GOD

FAMILY

This is the first institution God created, and as such is your priority and first ministry. Please plan for the protection and spiritual growth of your family. Make this a passion and do not leave this up to others.

> Deuteronomy 6:1-12: *"Now this is the commandment, the statutes and the judgments which the LORD your God has commanded me to teach you, that you might do them in the land where you are going over to possess it, so that you and your son and your grandson might fear the LORD your God, to keep all His statutes and His commandments which I command you, all the days of your life, and that your days may be prolonged. O Israel, you should listen and be careful to do it, that it may be well with you and that you may multiply greatly, just as the LORD, the God of your fathers, has promised you, in a land flowing with milk and honey. Hear, O Israel! The LORD is our God, the LORD is one! You shall love the LORD your God with all your heart and with all your soul and with all your might. These words, which I am commanding you today, shall be on your heart. You shall teach them diligently to your sons and shall talk of them when you sit in your house and when you walk by the way and when you lie down and when you rise up. You shall bind them as a sign on your hand and they shall be as frontals on your forehead. You shall write them on the doorposts of your house and on your gates. Then it shall come about when the LORD your God brings you into the land which He swore to your fathers, Abraham, Isaac and Jacob, to give you, great and splendid cities which you did not build, and houses full of all good things which you did not fill, and hewn cisterns which you did not dig, vineyards and olive trees which you did not plant, and you eat and are satisfied, then watch yourself, that you do not forget the LORD who brought you from the land of Egypt, out of the house of slavery."*

Set and schedule times for your family:

> Ephesians 5:16: *"Making the most of your time, because the days are evil."*

MORNING TIMES:

_____

_____

_____

MEAL TIMES:

_____

_____

_____

TRAVEL TIMES:

_____
_____
_____

DEVOTIONAL TIMES:

_____
_____
_____

BED TIMES:

_____
_____
_____

VACATIONS:

_____
_____
_____

OUTINGS:

_____
_____
_____

SABBATH:

_____
_____
_____

HOBBIES:

_____
_____
_____

SPOUSE DATES:

_____

_____

_____

SERVING TOGETHER:

_____

_____

_____

GIVING MONEY TOGETHER: (Teaching your kids to tithe)

_____

_____

_____

Please DO NOT leave the spiritual formation of your family to chance. Going to church is great, but it is not a plan. Hope is a lousy strategy. As parents, we will stand accountable for the kids God loaned us.

Does each member of your family have a Personal Growth Plan? Don't plan to grow yourself and leave your family behind.

FITNESS

"Your body is the temple of the Holy Spirit." ~GOD

"The better you care for your body, the more you can serve the Lord and care for the people you love." ~Pastor Chris

- Do you have a family physician? (If you do not, you will sorely regret it when a problem arises!)

- Currently, how would you rate your own fitness level from 1 to 10, with 10 being the highest rating?

- Do you get annual physical exams?

- What sports or fitness activities do you enjoy participating in and why?

- Does your family exercise together?

- Would you consider your family to be physically healthy?

- Does your family eat healthy foods?

- How would you rate your overall nutrition from 1 to 10, with 10 being the highest rating?

- If you had to select one thing about your nutrition that you could improve, what would it be?

Take time and complete the physical check sheet on the following pages.

Focus On Fitness

My Fitness Motivators and Health Benefits What motivates you to want to be physically active? Use the boxes on the right to check off what motivates you. Use the extra lines at the bottom to write down other reasons why you want to make fitness a part of your life.	☐ Have more energy ☐ Release stress ☐ Keep my heart healthy ☐ Improve my overall health and live longer ☐ Manage my weight ☐ Improve my self-esteem ☐ _____ ☐ _____ ☐ _____
My Everyday Activities You can move your body more by changing your daily routine, such as increased walking. Check off some of the things that you could change, and write in a few of your own ideas.	☐ Walking instead of driving or taking the bus ☐ Taking the stairs instead of the elevator ☐ Walking around while talking on the phone ☐ _____ ☐ _____ ☐ _____
My Other Physical Activities Other ways of exercising are physical activities such as bike riding or playing a sport. These activities require more of your energy. Check off some other physical activities you enjoy, or write them in.	☐ Bicycling, golfing, playing tennis, etc. ☐ Hiking ☐ Taking a dance or exercise class ☐ _____ ☐ _____ ☐ _____
My Time to Get Fit You need to make room in your busy schedule to include time for fitness. Think of ways to incorporate a workout into your day. Check off or add some strategies that will help you make time for fitness.	☐ Cut TV, internet time in half ☐ Take a friend, or a group of friends on a walk ☐ Schedule (and keep) workout time in my planner ☐ _____ ☐ _____ ☐ _____

My Fitness Goals Having clear goals can help motivate you and keep you focused. Check off or write in your top three fitness goals for the next month.	☐ Join a sports team or aerobics class ☐ Walk or jog 2 miles per day ☐ Try an exercise DVD ☐ Lose weight ☐ Start a walking club with friends ☐ _____ ☐ _____ ☐ _____

Fitness Plan

Day, Date, and Time	Activity and Location
Monday	
Tuesday	
Wednesday	
Thursday	
Friday	
Saturday	
Sunday	

"It is very unloving to abuse your body and get old and cause your family to have to care for you due to poor disciplines!" ~Pastor Chris

FORTUNE

Do you have any sort of financial plan for yourself or your family?

Complete the following budget worksheet, which is well worth the time:

Family Budget Planner

http://www.vertex42.com/ExcelTemplates/family-budget-planner.html

© 2008 Vertex42 LLC

Starting Balance	1500												Total	Avg
Total Income	0	0	0	0	0	0	0	0	0	0	0	0	0	0
Total Expenses	0	0	0	0	0	0	0	0	0	0	0	0	0	0
NET (Income - Expenses)	0	0	0	0	0	0	0	0	0	0	0	0	0	0
Projected End Balance	1,500	1,500	1,500	1,500	1,500	1,500	1,500	1,500	1,500	1,500	1,500	1,500		
	JAN	FEB	MAR	APR	MAY	JUN	JUL	AUG	SEP	OCT	NOV	DEC	Total	Avg
INCOME														
Wages & Tips													0	0
Interest Income													0	0
Dividends													0	0
Gifts Received													0	0
Refunds/ Reimbursements													0	0
Transfer From Savings													0	0
Other													0	0
Other													0	0
Other													0	0
TOTAL INCOME	0	0	0	0	0	0	0	0	0	0	0	0	0	0
HOME EXPENSES														
Mortgage/Rent													0	0
Electricity													0	0
Gas/Oil													0	0
Water/Sewer/ Trash													0	0
Phone													0	0
Cable/Satellite													0	0
Internet													0	0

Furnishings/ Appliances														0	0
Lawn/Garden														0	0
Home Supplies														0	0
Maintenance														0	0
Improvements														0	0
Other														0	0
TOTAL HOME EXPENSES	0	0	0	0	0	0	0	0	0	0	0	0	0	0	0
DAILY LIVING															
Groceries														0	0
Personal Supplies														0	0
Clothing														0	0
Cleaning Services														0	0
Dining/ Eating Out														0	0
Dry Cleaning														0	0
Salon/Barber														0	0
Discretionary [Name 1]														0	0
Discretionary [Name 2]														0	0
Other														0	0
TOTAL DAILY LIVING	0	0	0	0	0	0	0	0	0	0	0	0	0	0	0
CHILDREN															
Medical														0	0
Clothing														0	0
School Tuition														0	0
School Lunch														0	0
School Supplies														0	0
Babysitting														0	0
Toys/Games														0	0
Other														0	0
TOTAL CHILDREN	0	0	0	0	0	0	0	0	0	0	0	0	0	0	0
TRANSPORTATION															
Vehicle Payments														0	0
Fuel														0	0
Bus/Taxi/ Train Fare														0	0

Repairs													0	0
Registration/ License													0	0
Other													0	0
TOTAL TRANSPOR- TATION	0	0	0	0	0	0	0	0	0	0	0	0	0	0
HEALTH														
Doctor/Dentist													0	0
Medicine/Drugs													0	0
Health Club Dues													0	0
Emergency													0	0
Other													0	0
TOTAL HEALTH	0	0	0	0	0	0	0	0	0	0	0	0	0	0
INSURANCE														
Auto													0	0
Health													0	0
Home/Rental													0	0
Life													0	0
Other													0	0
TOTAL INSURANCE	0	0	0	0	0	0	0	0	0	0	0	0	0	0
EDUCATION														
Tuition													0	0
Books													0	0
Music Lessons													0	0
Other													0	0
TOTAL EDUCATION	0	0	0	0	0	0	0	0	0	0	0	0	0	0
CHARITY/GIFTS														
Gifts Given													0	0
Charitable Donations													0	0
Religious Donations													0	0
Other													0	0
TOTAL CHARITY/ GIFTS	0	0	0	0	0	0	0	0	0	0	0	0	0	0
SAVINGS														
Emergency Fund													0	0

Transfer to Savings													0	0
Retirement (401k, IRA)													0	0
Investments													0	0
College													0	0
Other													0	0
TOTAL SAVINGS	0	0	0	0	0	0	0	0	0	0	0	0	0	0
OBLIGATIONS														
Student Loan													0	0
Other Loan													0	0
Credit Card #1													0	0
Credit Card #2													0	0
Credit Card #3													0	0
Alimony/Child Support													0	0
Federal Taxes													0	0
State/Local Taxes													0	0
Legal Fees													0	0
Other													0	0
TOTAL OBLIGATIONS	0	0	0	0	0	0	0	0	0	0	0	0	0	0
BUSINESS EXPENSE														
Deductible Expenses													0	0
Non-Deductible Expenses													0	0
Other													0	0
Other													0	0
TOTAL BUSINESS EXPENSE	0	0	0	0	0	0	0	0	0	0	0	0	0	0
ENTERTAINMENT														
Videos/DVDs													0	0
Music													0	0
Games													0	0
Rentals													0	0
Movies/Theater													0	0
Concerts/Plays													0	0
Books													0	0

Hobbies													0	0
Film/Photos													0	0
Sports													0	0
Outdoor Recreation													0	0
Toys/Gadgets													0	0
Other													0	0
TOTAL ENTER-TAINMENT	0	0	0	0	0	0	0	0	0	0	0	0	0	0
PETS														
Food													0	0
Medical													0	0
Toys/Supplies													0	0
Other													0	0
TOTAL PETS	0	0	0	0	0	0	0	0	0	0	0	0	0	0
SUBSCRIPTIONS														
Newspaper													0	0
Magazines													0	0
Dues													0	0
Club Memberships													0	0
Other													0	0
TOTAL SUB-SCRIPTIONS	0	0	0	0	0	0	0	0	0	0	0	0	0	0
VACATION														
Travel													0	0
Lodging													0	0
Food													0	0
Rental Car													0	0
Entertainment													0	0
Other													0	0
TOTAL VACATION	0	0	0	0	0	0	0	0	0	0	0	0	0	0
MISCELLANEOUS														
Bank Fees													0	0
Postage													0	0
Other													0	0
Other													0	0
Other													0	0
TOTAL MISCELLANEOUS	0	0	0	0	0	0	0	0	0	0	0	0	0	0

Set Goals: _____

_____

_____

Develop a Plan: _____

_____

_____

Discipline Daily: _____

(Two good websites you can visit to get great biblical information: DaveRamsey.com; crown.org)

FUTURE

This section is the most difficult of the five most important areas for which to develop a plan. In this section the question is answered: "Why did God Make Me?" What is my purpose in life? Rick Warren sold millions of copies of his book, *The Purpose Driven Life*, which proves the question is on the minds of most everyone. The problem is compounded by the fact that most people do not like their jobs.

What is God calling you to do?

_____

_____

_____

Colossians 3:23: *"Whatever you do, do your work heartily as for the Lord rather than man."*

Somewhere we forgot the fact that we are all called to minister and to be a missionary. Your job or vocation is your mission field. God places us in our jobs to bring glory to His name and continue the restorative process.

What opportunities do you have?

_____

_____

_____

A PLACE TO START: (questions to consider)

What are your achievements?

_____

_____

What do you like to do?

_____

_____

_____

(S) Spiritual Gifts?

_____

_____

_____

(H) Heart? Where is it drawn?

_____

_____

_____

(A) Aptitude? What are you good at?

_____

_____

_____

(P) Passions? What do you care about?

_____

_____

_____

(E) Experiences? What experiences do you have in life?

_____

_____

_____

I would recommend Rick Warren's book, and also, *The Next Christians*, by Gabe Lyons. Thinking about your vocation Gabe said, "The spread of ideas—specifically, the Christian idea of restoration—will happen best and most powerfully when every channel of culture is leveraged. Keeping restoration isolated just to the church channel will only further separate Christians from the rest of the world. It's one explanation given for why parts of our culture have grown darker in recent decades. Christians separated and retreated, leaving a vacuum where others have spread their ideas instead. We 'left our posts.'"

About the Author

A gifted communicator who easily connects with others, Dr. Chris Stephens uses his unique experience and relevant teaching style to touch the hearts of every age group. Since joining Faith Promise Church as Senior Pastor in July 1996, Chris has been instrumental in facilitating the church's growth from 250 to almost 5,000 in attendance, and a staff that has grown from 5 to 50. He has a genuine passion to encourage, inspire and equip others to discover and use their God-given gifts, finding and fulfilling the purpose for their lives in the process.

Chris graduated from the University of Tennessee at Chattanooga, Mid-America Baptist Theological Seminary and New Orleans Baptist Theological Seminary with a Doctorate of Ministry in Evangelistic Church Growth. Dr. John Maxwell, founder of EQUIP and INJOY Stewardship Services, named Chris one of the *Top 40 Leaders in America.*

Chris and Michele, his wife of twenty-seven years, live in Knoxville, Tennessee. They have three children—Faith, Micah and Zac.

> "But you, beloved, building yourselves up on your most holy faith, praying in the Holy Spirit, keep yourselves in the love of God, waiting anxiously for the mercy of our Lord Jesus Christ to eternal life."
>
> **Jude 20-21**

Also available from Dr. Chris Stephens

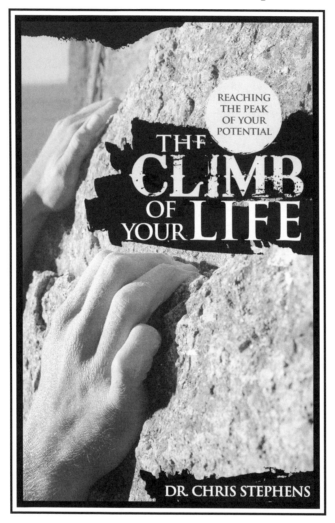

In this book, author Chris Stephens shares his amazing journey from a life in the projects with abuse, violence, drugs, alcohol and sex to his life today—leading one of the fastest-growing churches in America. Join him on the climb—discover the strategies that will help you unlock your true gifts and abilities to have a successful, fulfilling life. No matter where you are, you can always climb higher!

Available in Print, Kindle and Audio Edition at DrChrisStephens.com.

Order additional copies of
The Plan of Your Life

Available in Print, Kindle and Audio Edition
at DrChrisStephens.com

Faith Promise Church
10740 Faith Promise Lane
Knoxville, TN 37931
865-251-2590